*Gram
from Joyce &*
Christmas 1983

W9-ANZ-293

Homespun Gospel
The Poetry of
Walt Huntley

170 Gospel Poems

Homespun
Gospel
The Poetry of
Walt
Huntley

G. R. WELCH COMPANY, LIMITED
Burlington   **Ontario**

Most of the poetry in *Homespun Gospel* has been selected from Walt Huntley's *Homespun Poems*, Volumes 1, 2, 3 and 4. However, some new and previously unpublished poems have been added.

1st Printing 1981
2nd Printing 1983

ISBN: 0-919532-81-0

© 1981 by Walt Huntley

G.R. Welch Company, Limited
960 Gateway
Burlington, Ontario
L7L 5K7   Canada

All rights reserved. No part of this publication may be reproduced, set to music, stored in a retrieval system, or transmitted in any form or by any means without prior permission of the copyright owner.

Cover picture reproduced with permission of the Sinclair-Smith Press, Burlington, Ontario, Canada.
© 1981 Anchor ® — Dimensia® Worship Bulletins.
ALL RIGHTS RESERVED.

Printed in Canada

CONTENTS

I dedicate the lines I write
  To all humanity,
The rich, the poor, the humble class,
  The high society.

I dedicate the lines I write,
  That in them all may find
A Saviour's love at Calvary,
  True joy and peace of mind.

I dedicate the lines I write,
  That all may share a part
Of blessings that are mine each day
  And read what's in my heart.

Walt Huntley

ABOUT THE AUTHOR

Walt Huntley, popular Homespun Gospel poet, was born in London, England, and came to Canada at the age of three. As a teenager living near the Woodbine Race Track he was under contract to ride thoroughbred racehorses for one of the wealthiest and largest racing stables in Canada, the Seagram Stables of Waterloo, Ontario. His four and a half years as a jockey were filled with many thrilling and dangerous experiences, but he was happy and well paid.

Walt's prosperity, however, was to turn to something even richer when he was invited to a Paul Rader crusade. Up to that point he had never heard the Gospel, read a Bible, or prayed, but that special night he surrendered his life to Jesus Christ and began to reap a reward sweeter than gold.

Since that night Walt has faithfully served as a well-known Christian witness, Gospel singer, song writer, and poet. His Gospel poems are used and read throughout the world. Many of his songs have been sung by some of the finest Gospel singers: the late Mahalia Jackson, Bev Shea (Billy Graham's soloist), and Redd Harper (Mr. Texas). Walt is also known for his musical work with the King's Radio Quintet and Den Pascoe.

For ten years he managed Oswald J. Smith's radio studio at The Peoples Church in Toronto. In addition to his Christian work and witness, Walt founded the Toronto Steeplejack Company and worked on most of the tallest buildings in the city. This was also an exciting and dangerous career which involved him as owner and president for twenty-five years.

Walt often appears on 100 Huntley Street (Canada's largest daily Gospel television program), at The Queensway Cathedral, Bibletown, U.S.A. (where the well-known winter Bible conferences are held), and many churches and concerts. His scrapbook contains notes of appreciation from such notables as Ronald Reagan, Jimmy Carter, Gerald Ford, Robert F. Kennedy, Sam J. Ervin, Jr., Oral Roberts, and Pat Robertson (CBN — 700 Club).

FOREWORD

Walt Huntley is perhaps one of the most "outstanding homespun Gospel poets in the world today." His work is quite equal to that of Edgar Guest. There are a lot of people who can write poetry of a kind, but there are very few who have the gift of writing homespun Gospel poetry, and Walt Huntley has that gift.

His poems are always very human and very personal. They touch the heart because they describe the experience of God's people in a most realistic way. They are easy to read and understand. Their very simplicity makes them appealing.

I have worked very closely with Walt Huntley for many years and I know him intimately. He is a great friend and it has always been a joy to publish his poems. Everyone has appreciated them. He has a way of expressing his experiences that makes his poems real sermons. They speak for God.

Oswald J. Smith

Oswald J. Smith is that great and popular missionary statesman, author, hymnwriter, and founder of The Peoples Church, Toronto, Canada.

NOT BY BREAD ALONE

There was a time I tried to live
  On things this world supplied,
And after many years I found
  They never satisfied.
And then one day my hungry soul
  By faith touched Heaven's throne,
'Twas then I found to live this life
  Was not by bread alone.

There's something more within this frame
  That must be daily fed,
And not on things this world supplies
  But on the Living Bread.
The Word of God from Heaven sent
  The manna for the soul,
And all who feast upon this Bread
  Forever shall be whole.

This Bread is Christ the Word of God
  Who gave Himself one day,
A ransom for the souls of men
  That only He could pay.
And in such pain and agony
  Up Calv'ry's road He trod,
To die upon a cross of shame
  For sinners far from God.

We cannot live without His love
  Though hard as we may try,
For nothing in this world can feed
  Our souls or satisfy.
The lesson that we all must learn
  If we the truth would own,
It's only by God's Word we live
  And not by bread alone.

A DUMB OLE COUNTRY BOY

I'm just a dumb ole country boy,
  That ain't so very smart:
And when I talk I get mixed up,
  My gears are hard to start:
It seems I don't have many brains,
  Like other folks I know:
And when it comes to s'ciety,
  My dumbness there I show.

I tried to put the dog on once,
  I gave my boots a shine:
I pressed my suit and bought a tie,
  I sure looked mighty fine:
But when I mixed with that high crowd,
  My knees began to knock:
I stood there like an ole houn' dog,
  With all that high class stock.

I went down to the jailhouse once,
  To witness for the Lord;
I told them how the Lord saved me,
  They sure looked mighty bored;
They nudged each other and they smiled,
  I heard them say, "He's dumb,"
But they stayed in, and I walked out
  When leavin' time had come.

I'm still a dumb ole country boy,
  I hope I'll always be:
Just dumb enough to trust the Lord,
  For all eternity:
And so I'll just keep travelin' on,
  No brains and not too smart:
I'm just a dumb ole country boy,
  With Jesus in my heart.

MOUNTAIN MOVING

Lord, I've never moved a mountain
  And I guess I never will;
All the faith that I could muster
  Wouldn't move a small ant hill,
Yet, I'll tell you Lord I'm grateful
  For the priv'lege knowing Thee,
And for all the mountain moving
  Down through life you've done for me.

When I needed grace to lift me
  From the depths of deep despair,
And when burdens, pain, and sorrow
  Have been more than I could bear,
You have always been my helper
  To restore life's troubled sea,
And to move these little mountains
  That have looked so big to me.

Many times when I've had problems
  And when bills I've had to pay,
And the worries and the heartaches
  Just kept mounting ev'ry day.
Lord, I don't know how you did it
  Can't explain the where's or why's,
All I know I've seen these mountains
  Turn to blessings in disguise.

No—I've never moved a mountain
  For my faith is far too small,
Yet, I thank you Lord of Heaven
  You have always heard my call.
And as long as there are mountains
  In my life I'll have no fear,
For the mountain-moving Jesus
  He shall make them disappear.

THAT SOUTHERN CALL

Have you ever taken notice
  When the snow begins to fall,
Just how many northern preachers
  Seem to get "that southern call?"
It is either to Hawaii,
  Or some distant beauty spot
Where the sun is always shining
  And the temperature is hot.

Now—I know it's not the weather
  That these preachers would avoid,
These are hardy men of courage
  Full of fire—God employed.
All they're being is just faithful
  To the call, that's what they say,
And you feel so sorry for them
  When you see them fly away.

It's a terrible affliction,
  When you stop and think it through,
Leaving all these lovely snow-storms
  And the cold that turns you blue.
Just imagine how they suffer,
  Lying somewhere on the sand
In their shorts and coloured glasses,
  And a cold Coke in each hand.

This is downright tribulation
  And it nearly makes you cry,
As you gather at the airport
  And you stand and wave "good-bye!"
Lord, we place them in Thy keeping
  Let no harm upon them fall,
Give them strength to face each sunrise
  While they're on—that southern call.

A HUNDRED YEARS FROM NOW

Tell me friend what will it matter,
  Say a hundred years from now,
If you owned ten thousand acres
  Or just one old broken plough?
If you bought your suits in Paris
  And your shoes in Italy,
Or your clothes were made in patches
  Like the bed quilts used to be?

Whether you lived in a mansion
  With the finest broadloom laid;
If you had a private chauffeur
  Butler, cook, a nurse and maid?
Or if you lived in a cottage
  With your health gone on the skids,
Out of work and out of money,
  Just your wife and seven kids?

Sure on earth it makes a diff'rence
  What we've got and who we know,
Whether we are poor and hungry
  Or we're rollin' in the dough;
And if life down here was only
  All there was and that was it,
Then it sure would make a diff'rence
  For us all, I must admit.

But there's more to life than livin'.
  More for those who will believe,
More in store laid up in Heaven
  If the Saviour we receive.
Whether we are lost forever,
  Or to Jesus here we bow,
This is what will make the diff'rence
  In a hundred years *and* now.

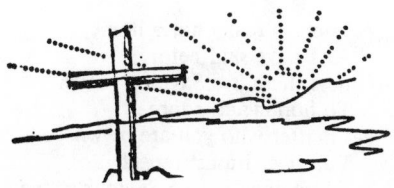

HEAVENLY COUNTRY LIVIN'

When I drive out in the country
  And I see those large estates,
With their lovely lawns and fences
  Swimmin' pools and iron gates;
What a sight of wealth and beauty
  On display for all to see,
Makes me think about the riches
  That the Lord has promised me.

Things eternal in the Heavens
  That shall never fade away,
Not like all these earthly treasures
  That we all must leave someday.
Things that eyes have never looked on
  Things that ears have never heard,
All laid up in store and waiting
  For the saints that trust His Word.

Ev'rything shall last forever
  In that city pure as gold,
Where the walls are built on Jasper
  And where no one shall grow old.
And the thing that makes me happy
  And to cause my face to shine,
Is no death up there to rob me
  Of those things God says are mine.

Talk about those country squires
  With their beautiful estates,
Wait until you see those mansions
  Just inside those pearly gates.
Then you'll see real Heav'nly beauty
  Things that time shall not erase,
And they're yours and mine forever
  Through the riches of God's grace.

IF GOD
SHOULD
GO ON STRIKE

It's just a good thing God above
  Has never gone on strike
Because He wasn't treated fair
  Or things He didn't like.
If He had ever once sat down
  And said "That's it—I'm through;
I've had enough of those on earth
  So this is what I'll do.

"I'll give my orders to the sun
  Cut off your heat supply
And to the moon—give no more light
  And run those oceans dry.
Then, just to really make it tough
  And put the pressure on,
Turn off the air and oxygen
  Till ev'ry breath is gone."

Do you know, He'd be justified
  If fairness was the game
For no one has been more abused
  Or treated with disdain
Than God—and yet He carries on
  Supplying you and me
With all the favours of His Grace
  And ev'rything—for free.

Men say they want a better deal
  And so on strike they go,
But what a deal we've given God
  Whom ev'rything we owe.
We don't care who we hurt or harm
  To gain the things we like
But what a mess we'd all be in
  If God should go on strike.

A
HOME
COMPLETE

A home is really not a home
  Unless there's more inside
Than all the things that money brings
  And parents can provide.
A home, though furnished as the best,
  With fam'ly ties so sweet
A home must have a Saviour's love
  To make a home complete.

A home that lives above the storms
  That life can send it's way,
Is one where those who love the Lord
  Can overcome each day.
No home is big or strong enough
  Nor mortals qualified
To stand alone against the grief
  That this world can provide.

When cares and trouble come your way,
  And knock upon your door
That's when you'll find how weak you are
  The rich as well as poor.
In times like these it's good to have
  An anchor firm and true
To hold you on an even keel
  With peace till storms are through.

A home is really not a home,
  As I have said before,
Unless there is a Saviour's love.
  To honor and adore
No matter who you are or where—
  You live, I must repeat
A home must have a Saviour's love
  To make a home complete.

THE CROOKED OLD PEAR TREE

It isn't much to look at
  In the winter standing there,
With it's trunk all bent and crooked
  And it's branches cold and bare.
Often it has been suggested
  That it's really out of place,
And just why we leave it standing
  Is a pitiful disgrace.

Cut it down, it's just an eyesore
  That's what people often say,
That old crooked tree is useless
  You can see it's had it's day.
I just nod my head and listen
  And at times I kinda smile,
That old tree to me is priceless
  And it shall be quite a while.

Wait, until the spring I tell them
  When you see that tree in bloom,
And the air is filled with fragrance
  From her blossoms' rare perfume.
And with fruit she's overloaded
  Till her branches drag the ground,
Then you'll understand the reason
  Why I wouldn't cut her down.

You and I could learn a lesson
  From that pear tree old and bent,
That it isn't what we look like
  Or the years that have been spent.
It is being fully yielded
  With the talents we possess,
And to those God sends the harvest
  Of the fruits of Righteousness.

WHEN LIFE BEGINS

When you reach forty years of age
  You've often heard them say,
That's really when you start to live
  For life begins that day.
I found that story isn't true
  Though some may disagree,
But this I know when I got saved
  Life then began for me.

I wasn't forty years of age
  Nor was I twenty one,
When God reached down and filled my soul
  With life in His dear Son.
A life to overcome by faith
  The tempters pow'r each day,
A life eternal and a hope
  This world can't take away.

You talk about when life begins
  And how old you must be,
Ask those who've found the Saviour's love
  Who once were lost like me.
And you'll discover all will stand
  And sing with one accord,
That life in all it's fullness came
  When they came to the Lord.

The greatest day you'll ever know
  What'er your age may be,
Is when your life in Christ begins
  And by His grace you're free.
It isn't waiting forty years
  To find the life that wins,
It happens on the day you're saved,
  That's when this life begins.

15

GOD'S
HALL
OF FAME

Your name may not appear down here
    In this world's hall of fame,
In fact, you may be so unknown
    That no one knows your name;
The Oscars and the praise of men
    May never come your way,
But don't forget God has rewards
    That He'll hand out someday.

This hall of fame is only good
    As long as Time shall be;
But keep in mind, God's Hall of Fame
    Is for Eternity;
To have your name inscribed up there
    Is greater more by far
Than all the fame and all the praise
    Of ev'ry man-made star.

This crowd on earth they soon forget
    When you're not at the top,
They'll cheer like mad until you fall
    And then their praise will stop;
Not God, He never does forget,
    And in His Hall of Fame,
By just believing in His Son,
    Forever—there's your name.

I'll tell you friend, I wouldn't trade
    My name however small,
That's written there beyond the stars
    In that Celestial Hall,
For all the famous names on earth,
    Or glory that they share,
I'd rather be an unknown here,
    And have my name up there.

THE
FRONT
ROWS

I often wonder why it is
    Whenever Christians meet,
They never seem to have much faith
    In any front row seat;
I just don't know the reason why,
    Unless they're filled with fear,
And think the safest place in church
    Is sitting at the rear.

It seems that somewhere down the line
    These front rows went astray,
Or else they're for those spirit folks
    Who always stay away;
They stand alone here week by week,
    I guess they wonder why;
If you were slighted like these seats,
    You'd break right down and cry.

Those back seats really need a rest,
    They've done more than their share,
The load that they've been carrying,
    It really isn't fair;
They never murmur or complain,
    They know it isn't right;
I wouldn't be a bit surprised
    If they collapsed some night.

Now tell me, friend, how would you feel
    When you with others meet,
And they gave you the same sweet course
    You gave this front row seat?
It isn't fair and that you know,
    So let's be kind and true,
And when you come to church again,
    Sit in a front row pew.

A
HUMBLE
LITTLE WOMAN

There's been a lot of mighty men,
  Upon this earth have trod:
Some seeking fame and world acclaim,
  A few have walked with God.
Yet I would like to tell you friend,
  Of someone I think great:
A little woman no one knows,
  With mighty men I rate.

She's just a little humble saint,
  With heaven in her eyes:
And tho' she hasn't got the looks,
  To win a beauty prize:
I'll tell you something that she's got,
  That puts most men to shame:
A love for those who've never heard,
  A dying Saviour's name.

I've watched her go to work each day,
  And raise a fam'ly too:
She doesn't have a bank account,
  Her clothes are seldom new:
She only has one thought in mind,
  To work and give and pray:
That missionaries of the cross,
  Help sinners find the way.

One day there'll be some great rewards,
  For those who've done their best:
To mention names I wouldn't dare,
  I don't know all the rest:
But when God's payday rolls around,
  Now don't you be surprised:
A little woman heads the list,
  With heaven in her eyes.

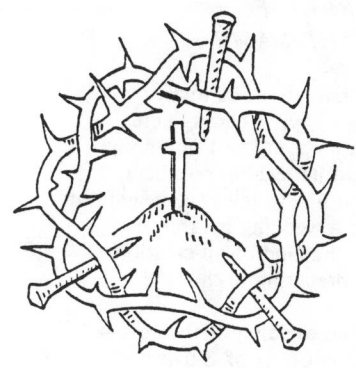

THAT DAY
AT
CALVARY

I stood one day at Calvary
  Where Jesus bled and died,
I never knew He loved me so
  For me was crucified.

And as I stood there in my sin
  His love reached down to me,
And oh, the shame that filled my soul
  That day at Calvary.

I knelt one day at Calvary
  My eyes were filled with tears,
To think such love I had refused
  Through all these wasted years.

And as I knelt I heard Him say
  "I did it all for thee"
And oh, the love that filled my soul
  That day at Calvary.

I prayed one day at Calvary
  I'm Thine for evermore,
Forgive me, Lord, for all my sin,
  My lost estate restore.

And as I prayed to me He gave
  Salvation full and free,
And oh, the peace that filled my soul
  That day at Calvary.

THE MARRIAGE OF THE LAMB

You may never be invited
  To a royal wedding here,
With its pomp and ceremony
  And its regal atmosphere.
So I'd like to tell you, neighbour,
  Of a wedding by and by
That the God of all creation
  Is preparing in the sky!

It's the wedding of the ages—
  Jesus Christ of Calvary
And His Bride—the Church He died for.
  Every sinner He set free.
What a Heav'nly celebration
  When the music starts to play
And the mighty Host is singing
  On that grand and glorious day.

Talk about a happy meeting
  When we gather in the air
And they spread the marriage supper
  In those banquet halls up there,
All the saints in robes of splendor
  Made of linen—white as snow.
There is room for ev'rybody
  If you really want to go.

You don't need an invitation
  And the price you pay is small.
Ask the Saviour to forgive you
  And upon His mercy call.
Join the Body of believers,
  Trust in God, the great I AM,
And someday we'll meet up yonder
  At the marriage of the Lamb.

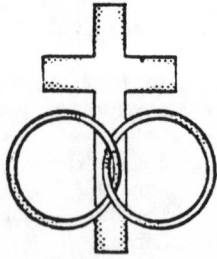

MY FRIEND O.J.

Of all the friends I have on earth,
  And I've got quite a few;
There's one I'd like to talk about,
  And introduce you to:
I've never heard him criticize,
  Nor unkind words display:
I'd love for you to meet my friend
  The one I call O.J.

He has no high falutin' ways,
  And yet he's dignified:
A stately air of graciousness,
  Flows from his heart inside:
You ought to hear him talk to God,
  And though his hair is grey:
I'll tell you this, the glory falls
  When O.J. starts to pray.

You never hear him boast or brag,
  Of all the things he's done:
And yet, I guess he's done as much—
  Or more than anyone.
To give the Gospel out to those
  Who've never heard the way,
I hope you've got a friend like mine,
  The one I call O.J.

I'll never lose this friend so dear,
  Who's been so kind to me:
For he and I will be good friends,
  For all eternity:
Yet while I travel here below,
  You'll always hear me pray:
"I thank you Lord for all my friends—
  Especially O.J."

18

WHY
I
LOVE HIM

You ask me why I love the Lord,
  And why I wear a smile;
You ask me why I feel so good,
  And ev'rything's worth while:
I don't know why He loved me so,
  Some things I can't explain;
I only know I've peace with God,
  And I've been born again.

It seems I'm in a diff'rent world,
  And yet it's still the same;
The diff'rence is I walk with God,
  Who died and bore my shame:
Just how I lived without His love,
  Is more than I can tell;
It's only by His matchless grace,
  I'm saved and all is well.

I never knew this peace before,
  Until the Lord saved me;
I never knew He loved me so,
  And died on Calvary.
But since my soul has been redeemed,
  My night has turned to day;
And now I'm walking in the light,
  And Jesus leads the way.

It sure feels good to be redeemed,
  To have this peace inside;
To know your sins are washed away
  In Calv'ry's crimson tide,
And that's the reason why I sing
  His praises here below;
Because He saved a wretch like me,
  That's why I love Him so.

THE
BOTTOM
LINE

In this world there's many seeking
  With just one thing on their mind—
How in life to be successful
  And for happiness to find.
Some are takin' up with business,
  If it's honest—that is fine—
For to them it's wealth and riches,
  Money is—their bottom line.

Others take up sports for action
  And they give their best each day,
Never satisfied with second,
  First, is where they want to stay.
They spend untold hours in practice,
  In their hearts there's one design,
How to beat the other person,
  Winning is—their bottom line.

We are all just individuals
  And our goals are not the same,
Still, we all have aspirations
  That to some bring world acclaim
Yet, forget the main attraction,
  That confronts us ev'ry day,
That success with wealth and winning
  Like a vapour, fades away.

There are everlasting values
  That we all should keep in view.
Things this world can never offer
  Or can take away from you.
Peace and joy with life eternal,
  Mercy, grace and love divine—
These, and for a home in heaven,
  Jesus is—the bottom line.

ROMANS
8:28

All things work together for good,
  Sometimes that's hard to say,
When all your hopes and all your dreams
  And plans have gone astray;
And though you cannot reason why
  Some trials fall on you,
There are some things hard to explain,
  And yet God's Word is true.

Most times we do the things we want,
  And God just tags along;
Then when we've made a mess of things
  We wonder what went wrong.
The truth is, we have not obeyed
  Or done the things we should,
And yet our God in spite of us
  Works all things for our good.

It takes a lot of faith at times
  To let God have His way,
So He can tear the idols down
  That we build up each day.
Sometimes we pay an awful price
  Before we see the light,
Still God has promised by His Word,
  All things will turn out right.

Things always turn out for the best
  When you are on God's side,
When you by faith have claimed His Son
  And in His death abide.
And though we may not do the things
  Or live the life we should,
Somehow the Lord will work all things
  Together for our good.

THE PABLUM BRAND

If someone should ever ask you
  Why some Christians are so slow,
And like under-nourished children
  They just never seem to grow.
Chances are they're on a diet
  And too weak to really stand,
For the pulpit where they worship
  Only serves the pablum brand.

How can any new-born Christian
  Ever grow to be a man
If he's always on the bottle
  Or the baby pablum can?
That's alright while we are playin'
  Pat-a-cake and peek-a-boo,
But to grow in grace and knowledge
  We need Bible meat to chew.

Something that will feed the Spirit,
  Food to nourish soul and mind,
This is what us saints are needing,
  Yet so hard at times to find.
And the way some preachers serve us
  When there's plenty and to spare,
Why you'd think our God in Heaven
  Had a cupboard that was bare.

Why not spread the Gospel table
  With some meat to help us grow
Strong to serve our God and Saviour
  As we journey here below.
Let us have a full-course message
  That will give us strength to stand,
And to those who need milk-feeding,
  Give to them the pablum brand.

20

HOW MUCH?

I've heard a lot of people say,
   When they were at the top,
They gave up ev'rything for Christ,
   Their income took a drop.
Some gave up fame and men's applause,
   And big careers beside:
I wonder what the Lord gave up
   When He was crucified?

I don't know where on earth you stand,
   You could be ten feet tall
But this I know beside the Lord
   You're really very small.
Just take your time and add it up,
   And see how much you gave
Compared to what it cost the Lord,
   Your sin sick soul to save.

I'll tell you, friend, what I gave up,
   A black heart full of sin;
I'm just a very lucky guy,
   For Jesus took me in.
I never was a shining star,
   A big executive;
I gave up nothing but my sin,
   That's all I had to give.

There's only One who gave up all,
   He gave His life as well;
In agony He gave His blood,
   Gave Heaven up for Hell,
That sinners, whether up or down,
   On Him might now believe;
You don't give up, God gives you all,
   When Jesus you receive.

NO EMPTY PEWS

If we knew next Sunday evening,
   At exactly five to ten,
That for sure the Lord of Glory
   Would be coming back again,
There would be a lot of changes
   When we all found out the news,
And next Sunday in the churches
   There would be no empty pews.

We would all be there and ready
   Like we were in days gone by,
When we lived at any moment
   We believed He'd rend the sky.
And I'm sure we'd put in order
   All the things we've done that's wrong,
And next Sunday all the Christians
   Would be back where they belong.

All this week there'd be such prayin'
   That you've never heard before,
And a lot of gettin' ready
   As revival fires roar.
What a night if God should spare us
   To be waiting me and you,
But we'd have to get there early
   If we hoped to find a pew.

Now I've only been surmisin'
   But I think it's true to say
You and I who love the Saviour
   Ought to live this way each day,
Then whatever hour His coming,
   Or next Sunday, if He choose,
We'd be ready in our places
   And there'd be no empty pews.

THIS
HUMAN
BODY

Did you know this human body,
  That we dress up ev'ry day,
Isn't nearly worth the money
  As the clothes that we display?
When they figure out the value
  Of our chemical contents,
All we're worth in U.S. dollars
  Is just over ninety cents.

That was well before inflation,
  Now since prices took a rise,
We have gone up more than double
  That I'm sure you'll realize.
Take for instance all the sulphur
  In this body if you please
There's enough to rid a houn' dog
  Of a real bad case of fleas.

Not to mention all the iron,
  Sugar and potassium
Phosphorus and fats and oils—
  That about makes up the sum.
All except one other product,
  Yielding more than all the group,
It's the lime—enough to whitewash
  Any farmer's chicken coop.

So you see this human body
  That we dress up and display,
Isn't worth a lot of money
  In a scientific way.
Yet with all it's cheap appraisal
  And the value they assess,
I'll just have to make it do me
  Till that new one I possess.

SNOWBIRDS

There's a lot of Christian people
  When the winter rolls around,
Head to where the sun is shinin'
  And no snow is ever found.
Like the birds they love to travel
  And when chilly days draw nigh,
They take off to warmer climates
  And to winter say—goodbye.

These are called the northern snowbirds
  You can tell them anywhere,
With their white shoes and sport jackets
  All so bright and debonair.
They're so happy to be livin'
  Where the southern breezes blow
Sure beats diggin' out a driveway
  When there's seven feet of snow.

See the ladies in their deck chairs
  Baskin' in the blazin' sun,
Like a barbecue on fire,
  Lord—have mercy when they're done!
While the men are at the golf course
  Shootin' eighty and below,
WOW! What a score—but they're not finish
  They've got nine more holes to go.

Well—it's time to pack the baggage
  All good things come to an end,
So it's back to where you came from
  And to those who call you friend.
But there's one thing that is certain
  Sure as Jesus shall appear,
All the snowbirds—"Good Lord willin' "
  Shall be back again—next year.

22

EVERYTHING
TO
LIVE FOR

He had ev'rything to live for
  And so much to make him glad,
He had wealth up in the millions
  And a real good name he had.
Ev'rybody seemed to like him
  And prestige for him was high,
He had ev'rything to live for
  When it came his time to die.

He possessed great fame and honor
  He was what the world called big,
In his circle he was headlines
  He was not no little twig.
There was nothing that he needed
  Nothing that he couldn't buy,
He had ev'rything to live for
  When it came his time to die.

All the papers wrote about him
  And they gave him quite a spread,
It would take a week of readin'
  All the nice things that they said.
It was such a lovely story
  With a "good-bye" at the end,
But it's only the beginnin'
  If the Lord was not his friend.

Yes—He had so much to live for,
  Wealth, and fame, and more to spare,
Yet, I wonder if he ever
  Planned his soul's eternal care.
If the Lord was not his Saviour
  Or his hope beyond the sky,
He had ev'rything to live for
  And just nothing—for to die.

THE
RECORD
BOOK

If all the things you ever said,
  Were written in a book:
And all your thoughts were on display,
  So all could take a look:
I guess there's not a living soul,
  Who wouldn't hang his head
And feel ashamed before the Lord,
  And wish that he were dead.

There is a record book I'm told,
  With ev'ry deed and word:
It even keeps the records of
  Our thoughts that can't be heard:
The good, the bad and ev'ry sin,
  For nothing has been missed:
It really makes me feel ashamed,
  To think what's on my list.

I know how far I've fallen short
  Of what my God demands:
And how I've failed my blessed Lord,
  With nail scars in His hands:
It's only by His wondrous grace,
  He listens when I pray:
When He can see my ev'ry sin,
  And how I fail each day.

And yet, the pages of my past,
  Shall never bother me:
For Jesus nailed them to His cross,
  One day at Calvary:
And now I stand in Him complete,
  Redeemed from sin and strife:
For with His Blood He wrote my name,
  Down in the Book of Life.

RICH
OR
POOR

I wonder what a millionare,
  Must feel like when it's time
To leave this world and all its wealth,
  With nothing, not a dime:
It must be awful standing there,
  When you have had so much:
And when you know you've only lived,
  For money, fame and such.

It isn't what you've had that counts,
  Or what you've left behind,
It's what you've done with what you've had,
  For God and all mankind:
For money has no value when
  Before the Lord we stand:
It's too late then to give to those,
  Who need a helping hand.

It's easy to condemn the rich,
  When most of us are poor:
But whether we be poor or rich,
  There's one thing that's for sure:
We better settle what we owe
  To God for Calvary:
Where Jesus died and shed His blood,
  For all humanity.

There's not a soul who ever lived,
  God's love could not afford:
It's free to all and without price,
  Faith in a risen Lord:
So if you are a millionaire,
  Or from the common set,
Invest for God in souls of men,
  And you'll have no regret.

PRAYER
MEETING

Did you know the smallest meeting
  That most churches have today
Is the meeting when the pastor
  Calls God's people out to pray?
From the largest congregation,
  Whether poor or well-to-do,
When it's time for prayer to gather
  You will find there's very few.

And we wonder why "revival"
  Is a word out of the past,
When the people came together
  As a church, to pray and fast.
But today, we've lost the vision
  Of the power we can claim
When we seek the Lord of Heaven
  In our blessed Saviour's name.

"Without me ye can do nothing"
  Is the warning of the Lord.
And success is only measured
  By obeying of His Word.
"If my people whom I've chosen
  Will be humble and will pray,"
Then our God has given promise
  He'll forgive and lead the way.

Prayer is really what is needed
  To be centered in God's will,
Meditating in the Spirit,
  And a life of faith fulfill.
If we all could get the message
  How important prayer must be,
As a church, we'd pray together
  Like a praying family.

IT'S SUMMERTIME

There'll be no evening service,
　The weather, it's too hot:
The preacher's gone a fishin',
　To a cool and shady spot;
The members they've gone swimmin',
　And the water it's just fine;
There'll be no evening service,
　It's too hot—it's summertime.

There'll be no evening service,
　The padlock's on the door;
Ev'rybody's gone away,
　Where there is fun galore.
The devil, he is happy,
　He knows that down below
There'll be no evening service,
　It's too hot for folks to go.

Now Deacon Jones is happy,
　He's lyin' on the sand;
Man, this is really livin',
　Just like the promised land.
His toes are in the water,
　Cold drinks are just a dime.
There'll be no evening service,
　It's too hot—it's summertime.

We all should have our pleasure,
　It's no sin to go away;
But Sunday is for worship,
　And for folks to sing and pray.
So when the weather gets too hot,
　Let's always keep in mind
We'll have an evening service
　In the hot, old summertime.

IF THERE WASN'T ANY HEAVEN

If there wasn't any Heaven
　Or rewards for me up there,
If there wasn't any mansions
　Or no robes of white to wear,
I would still be more than grateful
　For the life on earth I've known,
Trusting Jesus as my Saviour
　Since He claimed me for His own.

Knowing Him has well repaid me
　All along this pilgrim way,
Having Him to lead and guide me
　Has brought peace and joy each day.
Sharing in His tender mercy
　And His fellowship Divine,
This was more than I expected
　When He saved this soul of mine.

Ev'ry day I've had His friendship
　And His Word and loving care,
And in ev'ry situation
　He has heard my humble prayer.
If I never had of met Him
　Or had come to know His Grace,
What a life of dull frustration
　I'd have known and had to face.

As I said before I'm grateful
　For the life in Christ I've had,
Though at times I've had my sorrows
　That has often made me sad;
Yet I've had a life of blessing
　With the Saviour by my side,
And if there wasn't any Heaven
　I would still be satisfied.

25

DESTINY

Ev'ry day we all are working
  For the devil or the Lord.
We are building up our treasures
  For eternity's reward.
All our effort, time and talent
  And the things we say and do
Are recorded up in Heaven
  To be checked when life is through.

There are those who spend their efforts
  On themselves from day to day,
Without God to lead and guide them
  They just live in their own way.
And there's those who trust the Saviour,
  Striving hard to do His will,
Who have had their sins forgiven
  At the cross on Calv'ry's hill.

I don't know just where you're standing
  In this line that is so long,
If you've ever met the Master
  Or you're in the worldly throng.
There's a choice for ev'ry sinner
  And alone we must decide,
For nobody can be neutral
  We must be—on either side!

There's a crown of life awaiting
  If it's Jesus you will choose,
Yet if you refuse His offer
  Then the truth is—you will lose.
That's how simple is the Gospel
  And the message is so clear,
All our destiny is settled
  By the choice we make down here.

TWO
TIME
LOSER

Let's suppose just for a minute
  You and I could not agree
On the Bible or salvation
  Or the Cross of Calvary.
First we'll take your way of thinkin'
  That it just cannot be true,
Though it may sound good to others,
  Yet it don't get through to you.

So there isn't any Heaven,
  God or mercy, faith or Hell,
And all preachin' and all prayin'
  Is a waste of time as well.
Keep in mind we're just supposin'
  As we go to bed each night,
When we die that's it forever,
  If it is—then you are right.

Now let's do some more supposin'
  If I'm wrong and you are true,
If that's right we both shall perish
  I'll be just the same as you.
This is what you're always sayin',
  Yet if what I say is right,
I'll be safe up there in Heaven
  *While you're lost in darkest night.

You'll be just a two-time loser
  If your theory isn't true,
And I think that's kinda silly
  When salvation waits for you.
I don't claim to have much wisdom,
  But I think you will agree
There's a lot of stupid people,
  And they're not the folks like me.

26

THE
NEW FAD

There's a new fad in the churches
  That has got the men enthralled,
It's the answer to the problem
  When you're starting to go bald.
Just a cozy little hair piece
  That will give you grace and charm,
Make you look so fascinating
  Like a rooster on the farm.

You don't need to feel embarrassed
  Never mind what people say,
For you're really right in style
  When you're wearing your toupee.
But remember ev'ry morning
  When it's time the world to face
That you don't leave home without it
  And the waves are all in place.

All your friends will idolize you
  When this gorgeous sight they see,
It could put you in the movies
  Or on prime time on T.V.
All because you took the challenge
  With your hair receding fast,
And you bought a rug to cover
  Where your hair was—in the past.

Vanity is what they tell me
  In it all we've had a share,
But it's what a man is needing
  When he's losing all his hair.
Jesus knows our ev'ry weakness
  And from sin shall give release,
He remembers we're just human
  Though we wear—a small hair piece.

JUST
A
MISFIT

Ever since I met the Saviour
  I have noticed by degree,
Most of those I used to visit
  Now have little time for me.
Some will try to act so friendly
  And politely carry on,
But the message I keep getting
  Is—they'd rather I'd be gone.

Oh—they smile and they greet me
  Just like old time bosom friends,
But when I get talking Jesus
  Conversation always ends.
Really this don't hurt my feelings,
  For to Christ I must be true.
And His Name I'm not ashamed of,
  Even though my friends are few.

I have found I'm just a pilgrim
  And so out of place down here,
All because I love my Saviour
  Who to me is very dear.
I'm determined I shall serve Him
  Though some people pass me by.
They've got nothing that I'm needing
  Or my God cannot supply.

Big deal—so I'm not wanted.
  But that doesn't bother me.
I'm an heir with life eternal,
  With a blood-washed pedigree.
And when I cross over Jordan,
  Far beyond this hemisphere,
There forever I'll be welcome,
  Though I've been a misfit here.

WHAT A SAD WORLD

If we all were atheistic,
   What a sad world this would be,
With no faith in God of Heaven
   Or His Son at Calvary:
With no Bible to direct us
   Into Truth that we should know,
And no worship of a Saviour,
   And no churches where to go.

No Thanksgiving day or Christmas
   With the praise and peace they bring:
No revival times of blessing
   And no carols would we sing:
No Good Friday to remind us
   Of a Saviour and His love,
And no Resurrection morning
   Or salvation from above.

There are far too many valleys
   In this world to walk alone,
And too many disappointments
   When you go it on your own.
It is just a worthless struggle,
   And to be quite frank and fair,
When I had no God to help me,
   Life was filled with dark despair.

Without God there is no sunrise,
   And no golden sunset bright.
Without God no moon of beauty,
   Neither stars to shine at night.
Without God no hope or pardon
   When His love you fail to see;
If we all were atheistic
   What a sad world this would be.

ACCORDING TO HIS WILL

With respect to those who tell us,
   If we trust in God above,
Been redeemed and been forgiven
   By a Saviour's dying love,
That no matter what our problem
   Whether sickness, blind or lame,
If they lay their hands upon us
   We'll be healed in Jesus' Name.

That is true, no doubt about it,
   But there's one thing we should tell.
When we come to God for healing—
   There are times we don't get well!
That's no reason to stop praying
   Or our trust in Him fulfill,
Don't forget God has a purpose—
   All according to His will.

Ev'ry saint has got his promise
   And the Scriptures make it clear.
He has all our needs before Him
   So, there is no cause to fear.
If we know Him in His fullness,
   And upon His word we stand,
What's the use to fret and worry
   When our lives are in His hand?

You and I don't tell the Master,
   Or demand, what He should do.
He will never fail to help us
   And give Grace to see us through.
So, take heart and keep on prayin'
   When you're well or when you're ill,
And remember, prayers are answered
   All according to God's will.

THE GLORY FEELING

Have you ever had the Spirit,
  While you're praying, touch your soul,
And you nearly hit the ceiling
  As the waves of Glory roll?
Though you can't quite understand it,
  As in wonder there you kneel,
All you know is you're not dreamin'
  And the feelin' is for real.

This is something that is diff'rent
  Than you've ever felt before,
Kinda like you've made it over
  To that happy golden shore.
There is perfect peace and gladness
  As you praise the Lord above,
And your cup keeps overflowin'
  With the sweetness of His love.

Joy unspeakable and Glory
  Is as near as I can say,
For to honestly describe it,
  Words I know would not convey.
All the joy and all the blessing
  And the thrill that fills your soul
As you pray in full surrender,
  With the Spirit in control.

Oh' I know just what you're thinkin'
  As you look into my eyes.
This ole boy has lost his marbles
  And is chasing butterflies.
Go ahead, but you believe me,
  What I've told you is Divine,
Not just something you imagine,
  But is real and genuine.

FEEL LIKE A SOMEBODY

Do you ever feel discouraged,
  All alone and in despair,
Without any social standing,
  Very few that even care?
Well, take heart, I've found the secret
  That will give your life new tone,
Make you feel that you're somebody
  Like a king upon a throne.

Never mind the world of pleasure,
  Or the tinsel or its fame,
You inherit more than riches
  When you claim the Saviour's Name.
All your past can be forgiven,
  Take that load of guilt away,
Have the King of kings beside you
  Ev'ry moment, ev'ry day.

He will fill you with His Spirit,
  Son of God you then shall be.
Life will have a whole new purpose
  Full of joy and liberty.
It's a "rags to riches" story
  And it's wonderful to know
You are free—just like an eagle
  After being trapped below.

Don't you want this kind of Saviour
  Who can lift you by His grace,
Take you from just being nothing
  In His Kingdom have a place?
If you do, then come to Jesus.
  He will give you life anew,
Make you feel like you're somebody,
  That's what He will do for you.

THINGS THAT MONEY CANNOT BUY

You may own a gold Mercedes
  And a Boeing jumbo jet,
Be a magnate and a tycoon,
  Mingle with the upper set,
Own the largest racing stable,
  Oil wells and fame galore,
But, if you don't know the Saviour
  You're worse off than bein' poor.

Riches make you independent,
  Let you live the life you please,
But it's very poor assurance
  If you're dyin' with disease.
And when old age creeps upon you
  Or you're broken down in health
There is little consolation
  If you've only got your wealth.

Love of money is the culprit
  And the evil of the day.
It's the cause of many people,
  Without faith, who go astray.
And you cannot take it with you
  When you leave this universe,
There will be no U-Haul trailer
  Being towed behind your hearse.

What we need is God to save us
  And to fill us with His love,
Give us life that's everlasting,
  Set our minds on goals above.
Be not covetous, but thankful,
  And on Jesus' Blood rely,
For salvation, grace and pardon
  Are things money cannot buy.

DON'T LET GO

When you've had a lot of trouble
  And your faith is runnin' low,
When you feel you've hit the bottom
  And the devil says, "Let go,"
Well, I may not be a prophet,
  Yet I'll give you my advice:
Don't give up your faith in Jesus,
  Don't let go at any price!

Anyone can wear a smile
  When they've all they want and more,
When their cup is overflowing
  And success is at their door.
But it takes a lot of courage
  When you've tried to do your best,
And the breaks have gone against you,
  Yet you haven't failed the test.

Life is filled with many burdens,
  And our faith is often tried.
But, remember, we are pilgrims
  And the Lord is still our guide.
Sure we'll find a lot of sorrow,
  Disappointments, care and woe,
But our God will never fail us—
  Keep your chin up. Don't let go.

Don't let go your testimony
  Or the crown which you have won;
For the faithful there's a mansion
  When this pilgrimage is done.
Let us claim God's ev'ry promise
  As we travel here below,
Just a glimpse of home in glory
  Will be worth it. Don't let go.

FORGETTING THE PAST

If you've told the Lord you're sorry
    For the things that you have done,
And you know that you're forgiven,
    In the name of His dear Son,
You will never need to worry,
    Over anything you've said;
Once the Lord forgives and pardons,
    All your past to Him is dead.

You don't need to keep repeating,
    And reminding Him each day,
Of the sins you once committed,
    And how far you went astray;
When you've asked the Lord for mercy,
    And His Spirit dwells inside,
You are free and free forever,
    If the blood has been applied.

We are pilgrims on a journey,
    And the future is our goal;
All the past should be forgotten,
    Once the Lord has saved our soul.
We must ever keep on watching,
    With our gaze upon the skies,
With a hope that is eternal,
    That brings joy into our eyes.

Yes, the past has gone forever,
    "Praise the Lord, in Him we stand,"
And He's promised He will keep us
    In the hollow of His hand;
Let's forget the life behind us,
    Covered by the crimson tide,
And keep looking unto Jesus,
    Our redeemer, friend and guide.

A THOUSAND TONGUES

We sing, "Oh, for a thousand tongues
    To praise our Saviour's name"
And never use the one we have
    His mercies to proclaim.
It isn't hard when you're in church
    To witness and to sing
But when you face the world outside—
    Now that's another thing.

That's where the separation falls
    Between those who are true
And those who only sing for kicks
    Until the music's through.
The tongue we've got is big enough
    For praising God and self,
And if we had a thousand more
    You'd find them on the shelf.

Let's use the one we've got to start
    And see what God will do,
And if the need should then arise,
    Let's ask Him then for two.
I'm sure if we would start the job
    With what He has supplied,
We'd find our cup of joy complete,
    Press'd down and multiplied.

Not for a thousand tongues, dear Lord
    But loose the one I've got
To witness and to sing thy praise
    Whatever be my lot.
To worship Thee with all my heart,
    Help those who've gone astray,
And may my life speak just as loud
    As words that I may say.

IN
BUSINESS
FOR GOD

After you have been converted,
  Trusting Jesus and His love,
You should start right into working
  For the Master up above.
It's like going into business,
  Though to some it may seem small,
But you'll never be a loser
  When you give the Lord your all.

You should start each day out early
  As you read God's word and pray;
Asking for the strength and courage
  All His orders to obey.
You will find the opposition
  Trying hard to cause you grief,
But a little prayer to Heaven
  Never fails to bring relief.

God will never leave you wanting.
  You're the apple of His eye.
He's committed to protect you,
  And on Him you can rely.
No one ever has gone bankrupt,
  Or His blessings overdue,
When you're fully trusting Jesus
  What is His—belongs to you.

It's a wonderful relation;
  Father, Spirit, and the Son
Being faithful to your calling
  Guarantees the job gets done.
Though it may not seem important,
  And to some it may sound odd,
When you're sold out to the Saviour
  You're in business for God.

LIVING
DANGEROUSLY

There are many occupations
  That require lots of nerve,
And, to those who must take chances,
  All our praises they deserve:
Astronaut, and hard coal miner,
  Aircraft pilot, matador,
Submariner, deep sea diver,
  Steeplejack, and many more.

All these men, they live in danger
  As they go to work each day—
Just one slip and death is something
  That is never far away.
It's a dangerous way of living,
  But it seems, somehow, to me,
Those who have no hope of Heaven
  Live, by far, more dang'rously!

When you live without salvation
  That was bought at Calvary,
You are living on a trap-door
  To a lost eternity.
All it takes is that last heartbeat,
  And, if Heaven's not your goal,
That is it. No second chances—
  When you're playing with your soul.

Those with risky occupations
  Take precautions in advance,
Then, if anything should happen
  They at least have got a chance;
But to those without the Saviour,
  Unprepared eternally,
These are people deep in trouble,
  Really living dang'rously!

A HEARTBEAT
FROM
HEAVEN

We are living on the border
  Of eternity each day;
We are just as close to Heaven
  As the stars so far away.
And the only thing between us,
  Whether we are big or small
Is a tender, little heartbeat,
  Just a heartbeat, that is all.

Just a heartbeat from Heaven,
  Just a heartbeat, nothing more;
Just a tender, little heartbeat,
  Till we walk the Golden Shore:
Keep your lamp all trim and burning,
  Let it shine, you'll never fall;
Just a heartbeat from Heaven,
  Just a heartbeat, that is all.

In this land of sin and sorrow,
  Whether old or in our prime,
We are only just a heartbeat,
  From the grave at anytime:
No one has a lease on living,
  Any moment death may call,
It is only by God's mercy,
  That we live and breathe at all.

There's a place beyond the river
  Where we'll lay our burdens down,
Where we'll be with all our loved ones,
  And we'll wear a starry crown.
All our troubles will be over
  And no tears shall ever fall;
Just a heartbeat from Heaven,
  Just a heartbeat, that is all.

HAVE YOU
THOUGHT ABOUT
YOUR SOUL?

Have you ever stopped to wonder
  What this life is all about?
Why you're here and where you're going
  When your time on earth runs out?
Maybe you've been far too busy,
  Trying hard to reach your goal;
Would you let me ask you kindly,
  Have you thought about your soul?

You may reach the highest portals,
  And your dreams may all come true;
Wealth and fame may be your portion,
  And success may shine on you.
All your friends may sing your praises,
  Not a care on you may roll;
What about the great tomorrow—
  Have you thought about your soul?

Don't forget your days are numbered,
  Though you may be ridin' high;
But like all of us poor mortals,
  Someday you'll just up and die.
Your success and fame and glory
  Won't be worth the bell they toll;
Let me ask you just one question,
  Have you thought about your soul?

If you've never thought it over,
  Spend a little time today;
There is nothin' more important
  That will ever come your way.
Than the joy of sins forgiven,
  And to know you've been made whole
In the name of Christ the Saviour
  Have you thought about your soul?

ORDINARY
PEOPLE

As you check those in the Gospel
  Who unto the Lord have came
And have asked for His forgiveness
  Be believing on His Name,
You will notice not too many
  Of the mighty in that throng,
Most are ordinary people
  Who have sung redemption's song.

God don't want just individuals
  For their wealth and all their fame
Who have turned aside the Saviour
  Building up the fam'ly name.
He is looking for the weary
  Who are lost and need a friend,
One who'll lift their heavy burdens
  And on whom they can depend.

Yes—just ordinary sinners
  Without merit of their own,
Who will claim the Name of Jesus,
  As His followers be known.
Leaving all the past behind them,
  Walk the straight and narrow way,
Not ashamed to be His witness
  As they live for Him each day.

Sure, there's room for ev'rybody,
  Whosoever will may come.
No one ever is rejected
  At the cross of God's dear Son.
When the invitation's given
  And the tears begin to fall,
You will find most ordinary
  People answer to the call.

HOW MUCH
DID
HE LEAVE?

When someone wealthy passes on
  And friends and loved ones grieve,
There's always those who'd like to know
  Just how much did he leave.
It isn't how much did he leave
  For that is easy told,
For when we leave this world behind
  We leave behind its gold.

We can't take nothing from this world
  We're bankrupt on that day,
Our business here has closed for good
  When we've been called away.
With nothing to this world we came,
  And just as we were born,
That's just how much we'll take away
  When friends and loved ones mourn.

The things we thought belonged to us
  And all we called our own,
We'll find out just like life itself,
  To us, was just a loan.
We have no right to boast or brag
  And claim it's our reward,
For all the praise for all we have
  Belongs unto the Lord.

The only things we take with us,
  And this is wisely said,
Are things of faith done in the Lord
  That we have sent ahead.
The rest of what we have or were,
  And this you must believe,
Will all be left behind that day
  When from this world we leave.

34

BIG WHEELS LITTLE COGS

To do the work of my dear Lord,
    The Christ of Calvary,
Is greater far and means much more
    Than anything to me.
I'm not concerned in pleasing man
    Or in his favour stand,
It'd rather serve the God I love
    And know He holds my hand.

Big wheels are often dull and flat,
    And this you can't deny,
For most of them don't have much time
    For us poor little fry.
We're far too small for them to know,
    That truth you'll find is clear,
They'll pass you like a D.C. 8
    If to them you draw near.

But wait until God turns the page
    And all before Him stand.
The big wheels and the little cogs
    Up there in Heaven's land
We'll see if we are what we think
    Or what we claim to be.
When all in line we stand there with
    No partiality.

Thank God—I've got one title here—
    Just one that I embrace,
A sinner saved and sanctified
    By God's redeeming Grace.
The big wheels may take all the bows,
    But still remember this,
Without us little cogs around,
    God's way—a lot would miss.

PREACHIN' COUNTRY STYLE

"Oh, how well do I remember
    When the Lord redeemed my soul.
In a plain old fashioned meeting
    By His grace, He made me whole.
On my knees down at the altar,
    There I lingered quite a while,
Till His glory fell upon me
    I was saved in country style.

"Oh! that country-style preachin'
    With salvation full and free,
Nothing fancy, just the Bible
    In it's pure simplicity,
Now it may sound too old fashioned
    For the high society,
But that country-style preachin'
    It is good enough for me.

In this day of higher learnin'
    When we've risen socially,
And this modernistic preachin'
    Isn't all it ought to be.
Though it may sound high falutin'
    Yet it only makes me smile,
I would rather keep it simple
    In that good ole country style.

When I'm safely up in Heaven
    And I've got some time to spare,
I'm just gonna ask the Saviour
    Just how all the rest got there.
And if I don't miss my guessin'
    Just as sure as you can smile,
Most of those in "Amen" Corner
    Made it there in country style.

OLD FASHIONED THINGS

Men may say it's just old fashioned
  To believe God's Holy Word,
Say the Bible is outdated,
  And why trust a risen Lord.
Well—you're right, it is old fashioned
  Like the stars up in the sky
And the air and all the water
  And a time for all to die.

This old world is still old fashioned
  Like the trees, and wind, and rain,
All the mountains and the oceans,
  Harvest time, and food, and grain.
Truth, and honor, moon and sunshine
  And the blessings of each day,
Just like God—they're all old fashioned
  And that's just the way they'll stay.

Mother's love is still old fashioned
  And a baby's tender tear;
These will always be in style
  While there's men and women here.
Some may try to change the wording
  And discount our Holy God,
But, these things shall still continue
  When we're all beneath the sod.

If you want to know the reason
  Why we seek for change and plan,
It's because we all would rather
  Listen to the words of man.
God is true and never changes
  And His Word has made it plain,
All His Works—so called, old fashioned
  Now, and ever shall remain.

MOVING DAY

When you move into the city,
  Like some country folks will do,
What a change of pace and fashion
  That before you never knew.
All your needs are paid for monthly,
  Services and helps galore,
Daily papers, morn and ev'ning,
  And your mail brought to the door.

Ev'rything is locked and bolted
  With alarms inside the hall,
Just in case some thief or robber
  Comes to make a hurried call.
It's an easy way of livin'
  And I guess it must be said,
You're not "with it" 'til you wake up
  Sleepin' in a waterbed.

Yet, I'll tell you friend and neighbour,
  When the novelty is through,
There is somethin' kinda missin'
  As the walls push in on you,
And you get that country feelin'
  Of the life back on the farm
Where with all its backward style
  You could live with grace and charm.

Now, I've never been to Heaven
  Where I hope some day to go,
To that city built on jasper
  With its golden streets aglow.
That's the day when I'll be happy
  When I reach that other shore,
Never more to change my address,
  And my movin' days are o'er.

QUESTIONS AND ANSWERS

Do you want to know the answer
  To the doubt that you display,
All the questions and the trials
  That this world can send your way?
If you do, it's very simple,
  Take the Saviour and His Word,
He will make your life worth living
  And your faith He'll undergird.

Let Him speak to you each morning
  As you read His Word and pray.
This is when you'll learn the secret
  How to cope with life each day.
You will have a new direction
  If you trust and never doubt
How amazing all the problems
  That the Saviour can work out.

It's the only way to travel
  As you journey here below.
I have tried both sides of livin'
  And God's way is best, I know.
You can face whate'er befalls you
  And the cares that may abide,
With a peace and sweet assurance
  That the Lord is on your side.

There is nothing more that's needed
  If you're searching for the best.
God has made the greatest offer
  That through time has stood the test.
When you've got His Word, and Jesus,
  And His grace to see you through,
All your questions will be answered
  And each day He'll walk with you.

COMPLETE IN CHRIST

If in Christ you have salvation
  And His Spirit fills your soul,
If you claim His death at Calv'ry
  And His Blood to make you whole,
Then be careful of tradition
  And of men with vain deceit,
Who would say that your salvation
  Isn't really quite complete.

Some will say you need baptizing
  Once, or twice, or even more,
While there's others say you tarry
  Till you know you've got it sure.
And there's many, many others
  Who will tell you of their way,
That will get you into Heaven
  If you do the things they say.

Don't you listen to their nonsense,
  Though enticing it may sound,
For you'll find too many versions
  Of salvation goin' round.
Men who give you their opinions
  And pass on the things they've heard,
That just contradicts the Bible
  And not written in the Word.

There is nothing to be added
  To the sacrifice Christ made,
When upon Him there at Calv'ry
  Ev'ry sinner's debt was paid.
All the rest is incidental
  And it's worthy to repeat,
There is nothing to be added
  For in Christ we are complete.

THE
BEST
COUNTRY

Let me tell you of a Country
  That is free to one and all,
Where you'll never have to worry
  And no tears shall ever fall;
Want and fear, old age and sickness
  Never darken this fair shore,
Gold and silver have no value,
  No one's rich and no one's poor.

You will never see a prison—
  Not a drunkard will be there;
Thieves and liars, crooks and cheaters
  Will be missin' I declare.
War and bloodshed, disappointments,
  Separations and goodbyes;
There they'll need no undertakers
  For nobody ever dies.

Flow'rs will never lose their fragrance,
  It is summer ev'ry day,
Storms and earthquakes, germs and fever,
  Like the night have passed away.
Rent and taxes, pain and sorrow—
  And no cripples will you find;
Not a drug store nor a doctor,
  No disease of any kind.

Would you like to live forever
  In this Country bright and fair
When your life of toil is ended
  And you're free from ev'ry care?
Oh, then make your reservation
  Like I did and you'll receive
Your free ticket to this Country
  When on Jesus you believe.

THANK
YOU,
JESUS

Thank you, Jesus, for the good times
  That I've had in serving Thee,
And for all the peace and gladness
  By Thy grace, You've given me.
And I thank you for the lessons
  That You've taught me day by day
As we've walked along together
  On this narrow pilgrim way.

Thank you, Lord, for all the hard times,
  Disappointments, pain, and care,
And for all the times of sorrow
  All alone I've had to bear.
Through it all it's been a struggle,
  But Thy Word has been my guide,
Just to know in ev'ry trial
  You were always by my side.

You have been my Lord and Master
  And I've tried to serve Thee well,
All Thy orders I have followed
  As the books I'm sure will tell.
Though I've had a few misgivin's
  But, dear Lord, You will agree,
You—then others—have been listed
  From the top, then down to me.

Thank you, Lord, for this great honour
  That I've had to know Thy love.
Thank you, Lord, for grace and pardon
  And for all that waits above.
Thank you, Lord, for ev'ry blessing,
  For salvation, full and free.
Thank you, Lord, I'm just so grateful
  For the joy of knowing Thee.

THE CHRISTMAS STORY

On Christmas Day my thoughts return
  To Bethlehem afar,
Where shepherds, watching o'er their sheep,
  Beheld a bright new star.
I wish that I could there have been
  To hear the Angel say:
"Fear not, I bring to you great joy,
  Good will and peace today."

I wish I'd heard the Heavn'ly host,
  With all the Angels sing:
"To God be glory evermore,
  Glad tidings now we bring;"
To see that stable and that crib,
  The manger filled with hay,
And then to see the Son of God
  Who just was born that day.

It must have been a thrilling sight,
  Within those stable walls,
When God sent Heaven down to dwell
  Amongst those cattle stalls.
The wise men with their frankincense,
  The shepherds with their sheep;
And there within His mother's arms,
  Our Saviour, fast asleep.

I know my wishes can't come true,
  But this one thing I know,
My heart shall be His dwelling place,
  For oh, I love Him so:
And when it comes to Christmas Day,
  My all to Him I'll give,
The Son of God of Bethlehem,
  Who died that I might live.

PROFESSING OR POSSESSING

Could it be there are believers
  Walking here upon this earth
Who have never been to Calv'ry
  Or received the second birth?
Do they just accept the Bible
  And the teachings of the Lord
Yet have never been converted
  By the Spirit and the Word?

Now the reason why I'm asking
  Is because some people say,
All you need to get to Heaven
  Is to walk the narrow way.
That sounds good—we all should do it,
  But it seems a long lost art
And in fact it's out of order
  Like a horse behind the cart.

I'm convinced when you're converted
  You are saved and born again,
And the old life and its habits,
  Sin and lust, go down the drain.
Then anew we serve the Master
  Yielded, pure, and cleansed within,
Like a temple that is holy
  And a new life to begin.

Then we bear the name of Christian,
  Not by knowledge of the head
Nor by what some men are teachin'
  Or by what we may have read.
It takes faith and deep conviction
  And a drastic change take place,
To be sure you have salvation
  And to know redeeming grace.

THOSE
GOOD
OLE DAYS

When I go back in my thinkin'
    To those days I knew before,
When we had the horse and buggy
    And the five-and-ten-cent store,
You may call me square and corny
    When I sing and shout their praise,
But we all were much more happy
    Back there in those good ole days.

Ev'rybody seemed more friendly
    And the truth was more in style;
All you did to seal a bargain
    Was a handshake and a smile.
And if you should fall or stumble
    From the load you had to bear,
Helpin' hands with love and kindness
    In a hurry soon were there.

Church and Sunday were more sacred,
    And the preachin' was for real;
Sin was sin, and God was Holy,
    And the Bible had appeal.
It was read with more conviction,
    Not in portion, but the whole,
And before you fed the body,
    It was read to feed the soul.

Good ole days, they're gone forever,
    Never to return, they say.
They and God are too old fashioned
    For this modern world today.
But to me, I'll be quite honest
    With their slow and backward ways,
God was feared and more respected
    Back there in those good ole days.

ONE
OF
HIS

I'd rather be just one of His,
    And not just one of us,
Regardless of the church or creed,
    Though this may cause a fuss.
I want each day to do His will
    And know Him as He is,
It makes a world of diff'rence friend,
    When you are one of His.

When you adore His Holy name
    And love Him more than all.
Above the treasures of the world,
    Or pleasure that may call,
You'll find it's not an easy road
    And friendships will be few,
When you make Jesus Lord of all
    The things you say and do.

The church is good, it has it's place,
    That's where we all should go,
But only if the Son of God
    Is preached for men to know.
And all the Bible is received
    Inspired from above,
And where a lost and seeking soul
    Can find a Saviour's love.

The church can never save your soul,
    And that includes them all.
No preacher, priest, or anyone
    Regardless who you call.
It takes the Blood of Jesus Christ
    And faith in who He is,
The Saviour and the coming King,
    And I am one of His.

THE COMMON FOLK

The common folk who love the Lord
   Stand on a lower grade
Than those who choose the upper set
   Where bigger names are made.
They're satisfied the Lord to serve,
   Without men's loud applause,
And never crave for worldly fame,
   But live for Calv'ry's cause.

I'd say that most of those I know
   Are in the common class.
They are content with who they are
   And never by you pass
Without a handshake and a smile,
   A word of love and cheer.
They make you feel like praisin' God
   Whenever they are near.

Not so, with those who strut around
   As if they had it all,
With no concern for all of us
   Who they regard too small.
I'll tell you when we kneel to pray
   We all are small indeed,
When God looks down into our hearts
   And sees our common need.

A need to be what Christ would be,
   To walk the way He walked,
To trade our pride for humbleness,
   And talk the way He talked.
To follow Him in ev'ry way,
   No cliques, or special line,
And not forget we're common folks,
   Who for the Master shine.

BROTHER HENRY

Down in Mobile, Alabama,
   Where the fields of cotton stand,
There's the finest Gospel preacher
   That you'll find in all the land.
If you really want revival
   That will set your soul aflame,
Then you must get down to hear him.
   Brother Henry is his name.

When he stands up in the pulpit
   With his Scofield opened wide,
You can feel that glow from Heaven
   Start to burnin' deep inside.
And when he gets into preachin'
   With that honeysuckle drawl,
Let me tell you somethin' neighbor,
   He says more than, "How ya all?"

He's got truth you've never heard of
   And with proof you can't deny,
For the Bible is his witness
   And the source of his supply.
He just preaches what is written
   In it's simple plain design,
And as smooth as grits with gravy
   From the Mason-Dixon line.

Chances are you'll never hear him,
   So I'll tell you what I'll do,
I'll ask Jesus to arrange it
   When this journey here is through.
That He gets us all together
   There with Peter, James, and Paul,
And we'll all meet Brother Henry
   With that honeysuckle drawl.

JUDGMENT

I often try to visualize
   The days before the Flood,
How people laughed at Noah's ark
   And called him just a dud;
I guess they quickly changed their tune
   When rain in judgment fell,
And only eight of all that race
   Lived of the Flood to tell.

It makes me tremble just to think
   How mighty God must be,
For when He speaks in judgment tones
   There's great catastrophe.
It's happened many times before
   Through sin of wicked men;
Just wait and see, it won't be long
   Till judgment falls again.

You wonder why God gets displeased,
   And why He shows His wrath,
When puny men would challenge Him
   And dare to cross His path;
Well, let me tell you this one thing,
   Man's now gone far enough,
And if it wasn't for God's grace
   I'm sure He'd call His bluff.

Don't take for granted God's great love,
   And live in sin each day;
Or you'll be caught just like the thief
   That didn't get away.
You'll think all Hell has broken loose,
   Like those of long ago,
When God sends judgment once again
   Upon this earth below.

TEEN AGE WISDOM

Heard a little feller talkin'
   On a T.V. panel show:
He could speak on any subject—
   Nothing that he didn't know.
Just a lad not nearly twenty,
   Hardly dry behind the ears,
Yet he had a lot more answers
   Than Methuselah had years.

He knew all about the present,
   With the future and the past,
Education, sex and science,
   And how long the world will last.
This dear boy was really something,
   As he talked 'twas plain to see
He was filled with teen age wisdom,
   Yet he never got to me.

Once I thought I had some answers
   When like him I was a lad,
Though I never ever told him,
   I was wiser than my Dad.
When I think now how I rambled,
   And my thoughts back there return,
Most of what I said was nonsense
   For I had so much to learn.

You need more than just an answer
   To be right in what you say,
And a lot of years to teach you,
   For you learn along the way.
Teen age wisdom may be witty
   And at times may sound the best,
But it takes a life of livin'
   To find out what stands the test.

THE
ETERNAL
FLAME

Upon a lonely graveside hill
  In Washington, D.C.
There burns a flame upon the grave
  Of John F. Kennedy.
The President of U.S.A.
  A man of destiny,
A man of faith, unfailing hope
  That all men might be free.

He never walked an easy road
  To serve his God or man,
And when the going got real tough
  He never ever ran.
No compromise, he stood his ground
  For things he knew were right,
He'd rather die than let the hordes
  Of evil dim his light.

I never met or shook his hand,
  Like millions more I guess,
And yet, I felt he was my friend,
  My brother, more or less.
And then on that sad, awful day
  When hate was out to kill,
It fell upon this President
  And all the world stood still.

He's gone, and yet that flame burns bright,
  His name shall never die,
As long as free men keep their faith
  And on his God rely.
We've lost a brother and a friend,
  His love and smiling face,
And now he wears a martyr's crown
  In God's abiding place.

Eternal flame, burn on, burn on
  For all the world to see,
The price of freedom men have paid,
  Like John F. Kennedy.

WORSE
OFF
THAN YOU

You may think that you've had
  All the bad breaks in life,
And at times this may seem
  To be true,
Yet there's someone I'm sure
  Who is ten times as poor
And a little bit worse off
  Than you.

You may struggle each day
  And take home little pay
With the rent and the bills
  Overdue,
Yet there's someone I'm sure
  Who is ten times as poor
And a little bit worse off
  Than you.

You may break down in health,
  Never know fame or wealth,
All alone in this world
  Sad and blue.
Yet there's someone I'm sure
  Who is ten times as poor
And a little bit worse off
  Than you.

If you have saving grace,
  And in Heaven a place,
When the journey of life here
  Is through,
If you have this I'm sure
  Then you're really not poor
And there's millions much worse off
  Than you.

THE GOD
WHO
STANDS ALONE

On the day when Grace has ended
   And salvation is no more,
When the saved of all the ages
   Gather on that golden shore,
When the Book of Life is opened
   And the born again are known,
Who do you think will be sitting,
   God of all, upon the throne?

No—not Buddha or Mohammed
   Or the gods who others sing.
God Almighty, great Creator,
   Shall be Ruler, Lord and King.
He, the Alpha and Omega,
   Prince of Peace, the great "I AM,"
Who for sinners died at Calv'ry
   As the sacrificial Lamb.

Ev'ry knee shall bow before Him,
   From the day of Adam's fall,
Ev'ryone from ev'ry station,
   Rich and poor, the big and small,
Ev'ry sinner, lost or pardoned,
   All regardless of their creed,
Shall confess His Son called Jesus
   When salvation's Grace they plead.

What a day of jubilation
   When the courts of Heaven ring
With the harps and trumpets playing
   And the ransomed start to sing!
Unto Him, the Lord Jehovah,
   God of God's, who stands alone,
And forever and forever
   Reigns supreme upon His throne.

JESUS
TRAITORS

Is there anything degrading
   More to fall upon a man
Than to turn upon his Saviour
   Once he's claimed salvation's plan?
If there is I'd like to know it
   For it really must be low
When you turn a Jesus traitor—
   That's as low as you can go.

It must really burn your conscience
   While the Saviour you deny,
When you think of how you witnessed,
   Of His Grace would testify
Then go back to that old garbage
   In a world of sin and shame
Dragging with you ev'ry moment
   Guilt of Jesus' Holy Name.

I've got more respect for Judas
   Who committed suicide
For the selling of the Master,
   Who they beat and crucified,
Than those hypocrites and preachers
   Who, for wealth and worldly fame,
Have turned traitor on the Saviour
   After trusting in His Name.

Oh, the shame that they must live with
   As they go to bed each night,
All alone, out in the darkness
   Without hope or any light.
That's the price of turning traitor
   On a Saviour they once knew,
And I pray it never happens
   To the likes of me or you.

THERE
IS
STILL HOPE

There are times I get to thinkin'
  What a mess this world is in,
All because the devil's got us
  Bound and shackled, deep in sin.
With so many starving people
  When there's food for all to share,
And the crime and greed and violence
  And unrest is ev'rywhere.

Ev'ry nation is in trouble—
  Demonstrations on the streets—
Strikers—bombs—assassinations,
  (And those high-priced athletes).
Do you wonder why inflation,
  When you look around and see?
Millionaires are now as common
  As the milkmen used to be.

I don't see things gettin' better,
  That has never been the trend.
Politicians, they are human
  And they're standin' at wit's end.
Only those who trust the Scriptures
  And have comfort—peace inside,
Know the answer to our problems
  Is in Jesus to abide.

Man has failed to be the keeper
  Of this world, and all its need,
And we're headin' for destruction
  If our God don't intercede.
Surely somethin's gonna happen
  And to me it brings me cheer,
For the Lord Himself is comin'
  And that day is very near.

THE
LOSING
GAME

Have you ever tried to answer
  All the questions on your mind,
Why you're never free from worry
  And the trouble that you find?
No one seems to be excluded,
  You will find we're all the same,
And without the hope of Heaven
  Life is just a losing game.

All the poor, they have their worries,
  How to live and get along;
And the rich, they're not so happy
  When you hear them sing their song.
Kings and queens, they too have problems,
  If you only knew the truth;
Yes, the odds are all against us
  Like an aching wisdom tooth.

Now it may be my opinion,
  But the way I see this life,
There is very little laughter
  When you think of all the strife.
And the only consolation,
  After all is said and done,
Is the hope of God's salvation
  In the Person of His Son.

If you face the facts of living,
  You'll agree with what I say;
Life is just a great big headache
  For the most of us each day.
You may be the one exception
  But this truth I'll still proclaim,
If you die without the Saviour
  You have played the losing game.

MY CONFESSION

I'm not the saint folks think I am,
  I might as well confess;
There're many times I'm so ashamed
  Of my unworthiness.
I wish I were a perfect saint,
  And had no faults or sin;
And be like other saints I know
  Who all the vict'ries win.

And yet I wonder if it's true,
  When God looks from above,
If He can find one saint on earth
  Without one sin to love.
Or, are most people just like me,
  And need a lot of grace?
To be forgiven ev'ry time
  When they would seek His face?

I think if we were honest folks,
  We might as well confess,
There're many times we're all ashamed
  Of our unworthiness.
And when we stand before His throne,
  I'm sure we all will say,
We're not the saints folks think we are—
  Forgive us Lord, we pray.

PLAYIN' CHURCH

Some people say that Sunday sport
  Should never be allowed.
And those who give it their support
  Are with the devil's crowd.
I wouldn't know—I'm not the judge
  And yet, I'll dare to say,
That Sunday sport is mild compared
  To other games we play.

That playin' church is quite a game,
  We've all been good at that,
And when it comes to gossiping
  We sure can swing that bat.
We criticize what others play
  And how they stand and shout,
Forgetting just how many times
  Like Casey—we strike out.

We may look fine on Sunday morn
  With halo's turned up bright,
And as we meet to praise the Lord
  We're such a pretty sight.
We know just when to say "Amen"
  And how to sing and pray,
Yet only God knows if it's real
  Or just a game we play.

He keeps the books; He knows the score,
  His records are complete;
We can't fool Him—that's one thing sure,
  He's got us tagged real sweet.
We may condemn those Sunday sports
  Where all subscribers pay,
But let's be sure that playin' church
  Is not a game we play.

46

REWARDING DAY

In that land beyond the river,
  Just beyond the crystal sea,
There awaits some big surprises
  I am sure, for you and me.
Many things, so new and diff'rent,
  Not recorded in God's Word,
Like the great names of the ransomed
  Whom we've never seen or heard.

When the books have all been opened
  And our works are on display,
And we see the good and faithful
  And the price they had to pay,
True and loyal—men and women
  Worthy of the Lord they served,
With a crown of life rewarded
  In a section that's reserved.

Here, it's easy to be someone,
  If you've got a lot of charm,
And a little of charisma
  Never does you any harm.
But we better get the message
  That it's not our crowd-appeal
That proves Jesus is our Master
  Or what all we do is real.

So we all should be more careful
  Who we name as being great,
For, when we get up to Heaven
  God may have a diff'rent slate.
Let us pray for all the blood-washed,
  Mighty, famous, great, and free
For the Lord He'll introduce them
  When Rewarding Day shall be.

JESUS, NUMBER ONE

How I thank God for the lessons
  That He's taught me day by day
For His time and His direction
  As I've walked this pilgrim way.
I have learned to put my Saviour
  First in ev'rything is He,
No one else is more important
  For He's Number One to me.

When I felt His touch of mercy
  And the joy of saving Grace
Ev'rything and ev'rybody
  Next to Him took second place.
He became my Lord and Saviour
  And His will I've tried to do.
Ev'ry moment since I met Him
  He has been my Master too.

I had found real disappointment
  Putting faith and trust in man,
Risking peace and life eternal
  Without purpose and a plan.
But—when Jesus came and found me
  Walking all alone in sin,
Something happened, I can tell you
  In my soul down deep within.

Why should I not serve my Saviour
  More than others I hold dear,
When He gave His all to save me
  From my sin and doubts and fear?
This, I'm sure, has been the secret
  To the battles that I've won,
Always striving to put Jesus
  In my life—the Number One.

IT ISN'T
WHAT I
USED TO BE

It isn't what I used to be,
    It's what I am today;
It isn't what I used to do,
    Or what I used to say;
There's been a lot of changes made
    Since Jesus came my way;
It isn't what I used to be,
    It's what I am today.

It isn't what I used to be,
    Praise God! Those days are gone;
The mem'ry of those wasted years
    Just seems to linger on;
I can't deny the past, that's true,
    Yet this one thing I'll say;
It isn't what I used to be,
    It's what I am today.

It isn't what I used to be,
    Since Jesus saved my soul;
It isn't what I used to do,
    When first He made me whole;
I might have been the greatest saint
    That used to sing and pray;
It isn't what I used to be,
    It's what I am today.

It isn't what I used to be
    Before I knew the Lord;
It isn't what I've said or done
    Since I have been restored;
Those good old days, they come and go,
    Like us they pass away,
It isn't what I used to be,
    It's what I am today.

"THIS
IS
MY SON"

The virgin birth some people say
    Of Jesus isn't true,
He's not the Son of God they say,
    His father was a Jew.
That's just another devil's lie
    Straight from the pit below,
His mother said He came from God
    And surely she would know.

As long as Jesus walked this earth
    He said He was God's Son,
I don't believe He'd tell a lie
    Do you, this Holy One?
Who healed the sick, the lame, the blind
    And demon men set free?
Whose voice was master over death
    And on an angry sea?

"This is My Son" God has declared,
    And those who say He's not,
Stand guilty of accusing God
    And that is quite a blot.
They better have a good excuse
    As all the world would say,
When there before God and His Son,
    They stand alone someday.

I've put my trust and faith in God.
    My Saviour is His Son,
The virgin born of Bethelehem
    The pure and Righteous One.
The only name with pow'r to save,
    To cleanse and set men free,
The Son of God, the coming King,
    The Christ of Calvary.

DON'T BE A FOOL

You say you don't believe in God,
  The Bible is untrue;
That Jesus wasn't virgin born,
  He never died for you.
Suppose you're wrong, how will you feel,
  For all the things you've said,
For ev'ry time you've cursed His name,
  And for the life you've led?

You're mighty small to challenge God,
  I think you will agree,
When He has made the moon and stars,
  The sun, the worlds, the sea.
And you stand back to criticize,
  And say you don't believe;
I wonder what the Lord must think
  And how His heart must grieve.

You better start to mend your ways
  Before it is too late;
Or some day you'll wake up in Hell,
  That's Bible, plain and straight.
And there, throughout eternity,
  You'll weep both night and day,
To think you let the chance go by,
  And Heaven slip away.

So why not stop your unbelief,
  And give the Lord your heart;
Repent today of all your sin,
  For Heaven make a start.
And then you'll find His peace and rest,
  And joy you never knew;
When you believe that Jesus died
  On Calv'ry just for you.

A WHOLE NEW BALL GAME

When I first received the Savior
  Back there in depression days,
I was taught by good sound preachin'
  That I had to change my ways.
Cigarettes and booze and lyin',
  Runnin' with the worldly crowd,
Like theatres, were a no-no
  Since I to the Lord had bowed.

All the old things had to vanish,
  I was now a child of God,
And the road that I must travel
  Was the road my Saviour trod.
Any talent He had given,
  Freely I laid on the line.
Helping others find salvation
  Was the first concern of mine.

Things have changed a lot I've noticed
  Since the T.V. came to town.
Now believers are indulgin'
  In the things once brought a frown.
Even women priests and rabbis—
  Seems like all are in the act.
Black Jack dealers and bar tenders
  Claim their lives have been untracked.

Worldliness and compromisin',
  Never mind what be the trend,
Have no place if you're a Christian
  And the Saviour is your friend.
Yes, it's now a whole new ball game
  As they say—I don't know why—
Maybe times have changed our preachin'
  And we're gettin' Bible shy.

WHAT!
NO
DEVIL?

If you think there is no devil
  Like a lot of people say,
Let me tell you how to prove it
  In a very simple way.
Come to Calv'ry's cleansing fountain,
  Tell your friends just how you feel,
Then you'll find out if the devil
  Is a myth, or if he's real.

Once your blinded eyes are opened
  And the light comes shinin' through,
You will shake your head and wonder
  What a dope he made of you.
And the more you read the Bible,
  Study, testify and pray,
You will marvel how the devil
  Kept you in the dark each day.

Notice all the snares and pitfalls
  That he'll try to trap you in,
And without the Holy Spirit
  There's no way you're gonna win.
He is cunnin' and deceitful
  So be always on your guard
Those who underestimate him
  Wind up in sin's wreckin' yard.

All the saints know there's a devil
  And his presence never doubt,
For he had us bound in bondage
  Until Jesus bailed us out.
So if you want proof of Satan
  Come to Calv'ry's cross and kneel,
Daily live for Christ your Saviour
  Then you'll know the devil's real.

PRAYERS

Before I came to know the Lord,
  My prayers were very few;
And when I prayed I wasn't sure
  If any would get through.
Somehow I thought the Lord above
  Was always waiting there;
And if, and when I needed Him,
  I'd say a little prayer.

Like millions more of poor, lost souls,
  I wandered on my way;
No time for God, much less for prayer,
  Defeated ev'ry day.
I never knew the secret how
  With God to get in touch;
I thought you only prayed when you
  Had trouble—pain and such.

I still recall when in my sin,
  I often tried to pray;
And when I did, God seemed to be,
  Ten million miles away.
The heavens they were made of steel,
  And yet I wondered why;
When others said they heard from God,
  And I got no reply.

The reason why my prayers, they failed,
  My life was filled with sin;
I'd never been to Calvary,
  Nor was I born again.
But since He changed this heart of mine,
  And ev'rything is new,
I have no doubts now when I pray.
  I'm sure my prayers get through.

SHOW BIZ

If you call yourself a Christian
  Then don't be a hypocrite!
Take your place beside the ransomed
  And not where the worldly sit.
Get some backbone and be counted
  With the humble and the few.
Use your name to honour Jesus
  Where the saints look up to you.

Don't be like those Glory seekers
  Who profess that Christ is Lord
And to please the flesh are looking
  Still for fame and men's reward.
Don't become a show biz stooper
  Just to keep your rating high.
Come out clean and serve the Master
  To that old life say "Good-bye."

Don't get caught in all that traffic
  Where the world is pack'd in tight,
And those night club entertainers
  Are arrayed in grandeur bright.
If you have your doubts and feeling
  That it's worldly and a show,
Don't sell Jesus just for money
  Be a man—and don't you go!

There are far too many Christians
  Mixing with the devil's crowd
Where the thing that builds your ego
  Is applause for self that's loud.
If you claim you are a servant
  Of the Christ of Calvary,
You will find the world of show biz
  Is a good place not to be.

LEAVE IT WITH A SMILE

When I must leave this world, I hope
  I leave it with a smile;
You see, this world is not my home,
  I'm here for just a while.
I've no complaints with how it's run,
  Its fame is not my goal;
When I must leave this world, I hope
  There's peace within my soul.

When I must leave this world, I hope
  There's nothing that I've done
That I've not asked forgiv'ness for,
  From God or anyone,
I want to feel I've done my best,
  And life has been worth while;
When I must leave this world, I hope
  I leave it with a smile.

When I must leave this world, I hope
  My friends shall not feel sad;
Just keep in mind I'll be with Christ,
  The dearest friend I've had;
And though the valley to my home,
  Is only just a mile;
When I must leave this world, I hope
  I leave it with a smile.

When I must leave this world, I hope
  That God is pleased with me;
I hope I'll hear Him say "Well done,
  Come, Heaven waits for thee."
And if those left behind I'll meet,
  In just a little while,
Then, when I leave His world, I know
  I'll leave it with a smile.

SO FEW
WANT
TO DIE

There's a lot of preachers preachin'
 Of that Heavenly home above,
And a lot of singers singin'
 How it's filled with peace and love,
But, somehow with all that's waitin'
 In that Land beyond the sky—
Not too many praying people
 Seem too anxious for to die!

How we love to sing together,
 "What a glorious day 'twill be"
When from this old world of sadness
 We forever shall be free!
We get overjoyed and happy,
 As we stand and testify,
But we soon lose all our vigor
 When it seems we're gonna die.

Ev'rywhere you look there's sufferin'
 Pain and sorrow, grief and woe
Disappointments, fear and sickness
 Here, and ev'rywhere you go—
Really, when you think it over
 And the truth you justify,
Why you'd think we'd get excited
 When it's time to say good-bye!

But—I guess it's only natural,
 Though we love the Lord and pray,
To forget—to be with Jesus
 Is far better any day!
Yet, with life eternal waitin'
 And those mansions in the sky.
Let's be honest—just how many
 Do you know who want to die?

FAITH
AND
PRAYER

It takes lots of preparation
 When you're working for the Lord
And there's more than consolation
 When you know God's Holy Word.
But that's only half the battle,
 For the truth that you would share,
And it's only man-inspired
 If there isn't faith and prayer.

Prayer and faith, they go together
 Like a hand inside a glove.
One is just as much important
 As the stars and moon above.
Both are needed in their fullness
 To accomplish all our need,
Give us strength to gain the vict'ry
 Over all our foes succeed.

It takes faith to move the mountains
 That we daily stand before.
It takes prayer to give us courage,
 Peace, and joy, and so much more.
It is not in things we're doin'
 It's the battle lost—or won.
Have we prayed in faith believing
 In the Name of Christ, the Son?

We may speak with voice of angels
 And in Jesus testify,
But, the proof is in the puddin'
 Is there fruit to justify?
It may be a shock to many
 But the truth to all I'll share,
All our hopes are next to nothing
 If there isn't faith and prayer.

IT
IS
WRITTEN

If it wasn't for the Bible
  That I read day after day
And the Holy Spirit's teaching
  That I ask for when I pray,
I would sure be in a muddle
  With the things I hear and see,
If I never had the Scriptures,
  How confusing it would be!

What with all the modern versions
  Of the Word of God I read
And the books that they are selling
  To explain the truth I need,
Makes me wonder how the Christians
  Ever trusted long ago,
When they took the Word as final
  And by faith believed it so.

What has brought about the changes
  In the Church of Christ today?
Has the message lost its meaning
  And God's truth is in decay?
Seems to me we're deep in trouble,
  Those of us who know the Lord,
If we don't get back to basics
  We shall reap a sad reward.

It is written—plain and simple,
  Undeniable and true,
Without error—undefiled,
  Never mind what man may do.
Though they modernize its meaning
  With some choice alternatives,
They can never change its message
  Not as long as God still lives.

BORN
AGAIN

Once the sermon has been finished
  And the Gospel has been spread,
When the altar call is over
  And the last "Amen" is said,
Weary souls have been converted,
  Many new lives have begun,
It's a day of great beginnings
  And the victory is won!

All the past is now forgiven,
  You are saved by Grace Divine.
By His Spirit you are baptized
  And can say "The Lord is mine."
You have made a big decision,
  There is peace and joy inside,
All your shackles have been broken
  Through the blood of Calv'ry's tide.

This is something supernatural,
  How it happens, no one knows,
But there is this sweet assurance
  That it's real as when it snows.
All the old things that you craved for
  And defeated you each day,
Never more shall be your master,
  Now the Saviour holds full sway.

Born again—Oh, what a wonder!
  It's so beautiful and true.
You just feel so clean all over
  And as fresh as morning dew.
This is only just a foretaste
  Of eternal things in store,
You are now a new creation
  Born again—forevermore!

DON'T IT MAKE YOU FEEL SO SMALL?

When you see God's great creation,
　As you look around each day,
Just to think that He from nothing
　Made and put it on display.
Ev'rything in place and order—
　Land, and sea and mountains tall.
When you stop and think it over
　Don't it make you feel so small?

All the stars up in the Heavens
　Far beyond the count of man,
Sun and moon held there by nothing.
　Figure that one—if you can.
All of nature that surrounds us
　Winter, summer, spring and fall,
When you really get the picture
　Don't it make you feel so small?

Still there are some little sinners
　Who just won't give God His due,
And they get uptight and bothered
　When you claim it must be true.
As you stand in awe and wonder
　Of Almighty God's great plan,
Giving life to every creature
　And a hope for every man.

When you think of His salvation,
　Sending Jesus down to earth
From the Golden Halls of Heaven
　To a humble manger birth.
And for all His Grace and Mercy
　Offered free to one and all
Let me ask you—now be honest.
　Don't it make you feel so small?

PASTOR SAM

In the little town of Grassie,
　Near a place called Stoney Creek,
There you'll find a country preacher
　With a spiritual physique.
Not a man of many letters
　But, a saint who loves the Lord.
He is out and out for Jesus
　Nothing less can he afford.

He's an easy-goin' preacher
　Who can sing a song for you,
Play the fiddle and the guitar,
　And the five-string banjo too.
He's a man of many talents
　Yet, he's careful to admit
What he is or ever shall be
　Is by grace—and that is it.

Nothin' fancy in his preachin'
　Just the truth you can't deny.
He can lift you from the valley
　To the mountain tops on high.
Jesus is his Lord and Master
　And no guile in him is found.
He's in business for the Saviour,
　Without any foolin' 'round.

Pastor Sam is what they call him—
　Just a sinner saved by grace.
You can tell he loves the Saviour
　By the smile upon his face.
Sam is one of those dear people
　Who is special and unique,
And you'll find him there in Grassie
　Near a place called Stoney Creek.

THE COST
OF
SALVATION

Don't you ever think salvation,
  That is offered free to all,
Is just something with no value
  Or the cost for it was small?
If you do, then you're mistaken
  And as wrong as wrong can be,
For the wealth of all the ages
  Couldn't pay for Calvary.

It has cost the Lord of Heaven
  Ev'rything this gulf to span,
With His life and all His Glory
  When He died for sinful man.
Born and cradled in a stable
  In the midst of poverty,
Oh, what low humiliation,
  For the Son of God was He.

Then to walk the hills and valleys
  With no place to lay His head,
Always looking after others,
  Seeing that the poor were fed.
God had sent Him here to suffer
  On a Cross to pay for sin,
And they whipped Him without mercy,
  Then the nails were driven in.

Wrath and judgment, pain and sorrow,
  Body bleeding, marred, forlorn,
There He hung without a murmur
  As the clothes from Him were torn.
Then He cried out, "It is finished"
  For a world of sinner's lost:
He had paid in full the ransom,
  That is what salvation cost.

YOU CAN
ALWAYS
START AGAIN

Once you may have had the fullness
  Of redemption in your soul,
Once you may have been rejoicing
  With the Saviour in control:
If somehow you've lost the blessing
  And you're on a lower plane,
Don't forget there's always pardon;
  You can always start again.

No one's big enough to carry
  All the burdens and the care
That in life we all must suffer
  Without failing here or there,
And when we let circumstances
  Override and get us down,
That is when we lose the glory
  Of the overcomer's crown.

Yet with all our faults and failures
  And our wand'ring from the fold,
God in mercy still He loves us
  Though our hearts are hard and cold—
And He's always ready waiting
  To forgive and vindicate
All who call on Him as Saviour,
  And the crooked paths make straight.

Never mind how far you've fallen
  Or how deep the rut you're in,
All the past can be forgiven,
  You a new life can begin,
Though your sins be read as crimson
  And your life seems all in vain,
Don't forget there's always pardon;
  You can always start again.

CALVARY

Calvary, or dark Golgotha,
  Is the place where Jesus died.
There between two thieves He suffered
  And for sin was crucified.
Lamb of God, without a blemish,
  Nailed upon a cross was He,
To redeem a world in darkness
  That all sinners might go free.

Three dark hours of shame and torment,
  Mocking crowds all standing by,
Taking out their vent and feelings
  As they slowly watched Him die.
All because He was the Saviour
  Who from Heaven God had sent,
Giving hope and full salvation
  To all those who would repent.

Scarred and wounded was His Body
  As a cross He gladly bore,
Marred beyond the sight of reason
  As His flesh was pierced and tore.
Not a very pretty picture,
  But the truth can't be denied.
No one really can describe it
  Or just how that Jesus died.

What He did, He did it freely
  To redeem a fallen race.
He alone could be the Saviour,
  No one else could fill that place.
That's the reason why I love Him.
  By His death He set me free,
When He gave His life a ransom
  At a place, called Calvary.

FIRST LOVE

When I first came to the Saviour
  There was much I had to learn;
Though I never knew the Scriptures
  I had energy to burn.
Ev'ry day I tried to witness
  To my friends and those I'd meet,
And I often sang His praises
  At the corner of the street.

I was grateful for salvation
  When it dawned upon my soul,
That the Lord was now my Saviour
  And His Blood had made me whole.
Though I never could explain it,
  All I knew 'twas from above;
This was something more than feeling,
  This was really my first love.

My first love for Christ my Saviour
  Who had died to ransom me,
Who had broken Satan's pow'r
  And from sin had set me free.
People shook their heads in pity
  And they said it wouldn't last,
And I'd soon come back to normal
  When the thrill was gone and past.

All these years this love has lasted,
  And it's just as real today
As the moment I met Jesus
  And the old things passed away.
And until He calls me yonder
  To those mansions up above,
I just pray the Lord will keep me
  By His grace in my first love.

THE OLD CHURCH

The old church stood a hundred years
  And had that musty smell,
The outside really was a mess,
  The inside just as well.
The pastor and the board agreed
  That now that it was old,
And what with prices up so high
  The old church should be sold.

And so they sold it and they built
  A new church with some class,
With offices and carpet floors
  Oak pews and leaded glass.
The lighting now was indirect
  The nurs'ry pink and blue,
And sep'rate rooms for all the staff
  All air conditioned too.

The parkin' lot was paved and marked.
  Each car has got a space,
And for a few important ones
  A sign reserves their place.
You must admit it's well equipped
  And lovely, I declare,
As any new church you will find
  On this earth anywhere.

And yet, somehow with all it's class
  And all it's new appeal,
There's something missin' seems to me,
  That made that old church real.
Or maybe I'm just gettin' old
  Or just too blind to see
The new church ever being what
  The old church used to be.

SUPPOSIN'

Supposin' that the atheists
  Were right in what they say;
No everlasting life above,
  No God, no judgment day;
Supposin' that this life was all,
  And when it's done we're through;
The Christian hasn't lost a thing
  If all of this were true.

Supposin' that we lived your way,
  No God to love or care,
No Christ to take our burdens to,
  No hope, no faith, no pray'r;
Just eat and drink and do your best,
  Then die just like a dog;
To live that way is dangerous,
  Like driving in a fog.

Supposin' that there is a God,
  And when the day is done,
What will you say when there you stand
  Before Him and His Son?
It's too late then to kneel and pray
  Too late to change your mind,
Too late for all eternity,
  Too late His grace to find.

Supposin' isn't good enough.
  There's still a better way;
To know for sure that God is real
  Is possible today;
It only takes just simple faith
  To cleanse you from your sin,
To let you know there is a God,
  He'll dwell Himself within.

EASTER

Easter is a time of sorrow
  And some bitter memories,
When the Lord of Heaven suffered
  Just to please His enemies.
First, they took Him from the garden,
  Then to Pilate's judgment hall,
To accuse Him like a sinner
  Without any cause at all.

There they scourged and beat His body
  For the good that He had done.
He had told them plain and frankly
  He was God's beloved Son.
Roman soldiers were His captors,
  Pilate knew that he was wrong
Yet, He gave the Lord of Glory
  Over to an angry throng.

After this they stood and mocked Him
  And a cross they made Him bear.
Up a hill that leads to Calv'ry,
  Crown of thorns they made Him wear.
There between two thieves they nailed Him,
  Pierced His hands—His feet—and side
To redeem a world of sinners.
  That's the reason Jesus died.

In a borrowed tomb they laid Him.
  It was guarded night and day.
Death could no more hold the Saviour,
  Soon the stone was rolled away.
He arose in mighty triumph
  For His dying days were o'er—
With His blood He paid the ransom.
  Now He lives—forevermore.

IT'S NOT EASY

Did you think to live for Jesus
  Was some simple little thing,
Like a lot of people tell us
  And a lot of others sing?
If you did, then you need someone
  Who will tell you what is true,
That for Born Again believers
  It's a struggle all life through.

You will find, when you're confessing
  Christ before the world each day,
You'll be just about as welcome
  As a bale of mouldy hay.
All the world will leave you friendless
  And they'll give you lots of room,
Just as if you had the measles
  And your spots were all in bloom.

Those who find it very easy
  Just to live the Christian life
Without any persecution,
  Loneliness, and grief, and strife,
Must be reading something diff'rent
  From the Bible that I've got—
Or they have a tongue-tied witness
  And a spine that bends a lot.

If we have no tribulation
  And the world thinks we are great,
Then according to the Scriptures
  We're just in one awful state!
For to witness for the Master,
  With a testimony clear,
You will find it's not that easy
  As you serve the Saviour here.

NO CHURCH SAVES

If you're just a good church member
  Chances are you'll go to Hell,
This includes the Roman Catholic
  Greek, and Protestant as well,
And regardless of your thinkin'
  Or the shock that this may be,
There is not one church can save you
  Or from sin can set you free.

This is really quite a statement,
  And if you should think me wrong,
I could prove it with the Bible
  And it wouldn't take me long.
Churches, like denominations,
  May appear to be the same,
But for mercy, grace and pardon
  You must call on Jesus' name.

Not a church but in a person,
  He alone can save your soul,
It is Jesus Christ the Saviour,
  Only He can make you whole.
Faith in Him, His blood to cleanse you
  And your past to all erase,
This is what it takes to save you,
  And no church can take its place.

Have you ever asked the question
  What must I do to be saved?
If you have, there's just one answer
  That in Blood has been engraved.
God has made it very simple,
  If His child you would be,
You must come in faith believing,
  To His Son at Calvary.

WITNESSING

Are you one of those dear people
  Who believes it doesn't pay
To tell others you're a Christian,
  That your sins are washed away?
Do you feel it isn't proper
  To reveal salvation's plan,
And when sinners curse the Saviour
  You close up just like a clam?

Don't you think that those around you
  Should be told of saving grace,
Or how you became converted
  And how Jesus took your place?
Or somehow is it a secret
  That to others you won't tell,
While you're on your way to Heaven
  They are on their way to Hell?

Don't you sometimes feel quite guilty
  With the ones you meet each day,
Or when some dear friend or loved one
  Who in sin has passed away?
Just to think you could have helped them
  Or to just have testified
That in Christ there was salvation
  And in Him they could have died.

If it hadn't been for someone,
  Chances are I'd still be lost,
And the same applies to others
  If I fail to pay the cost.
Just a word for Christ won't break me,
  And at least one thing I'll know,
I'll be pleasing my dear Saviour
  Witnessing for Him below.

PRESENT
WITH
THE LORD

To be absent from the body,
  To be present with the Lord,
That's the promise of the Scriptures
  For the saints who trust its word.
When the spirit leaves the body
  And to Heaven wings its flight,
Safe, forever, with the Saviour
  In that land where there's no night.

No more worry, fears or heartaches
  When this world we leave behind,
From all earthly toil and struggle,
  Joy and peace and rest to find.
To be ever free from trouble
  And the burdens here below,
All our friends and all our loved ones
  We shall meet again and know.

Pain and grief shall all be ended,
  God shall wipe away all tears,
There to worship and to serve Him
  Where there is no time or years.
By His side through endless ages,
  All shall live in harmony,
When the journey here is over
  And we're in eternity.

What a day to be with Jesus,
  Never more to walk alone,
Face to face with Him who loved us
  And redeemed us for His own.
Death is only the beginning
  Of a life with sweet accord,
To be absent from the body,
  To be present with the Lord.

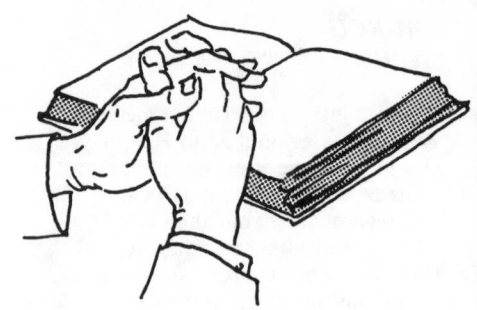

FAITH

Faith has only got five letters,
  F A I T H —that's all,
And beside most other wording
  It's comparatively small.
Yet, with all its small dimension,
  When you claim this mighty word,
All the pow'r of Heav'n is waiting
  When you use it in the Lord.

Faith makes things that are unpleasant
  And impossible to gain
All come true—just like the sunshine—
  When you call on Jesus' name.
Just a little word, so potent,
  That regardless of your need
It will win each losing battle
  And your fondest hopes exceed.

When you're in a heap of trouble
  And you don't know what to do,
Talk to God, in faith believing,
  He will always see you through.
Never mind how deep the valley
  Or the turmoil that you're in,
Faith will put you on the mountain,
  Give you peace, and make you win.

Life is filled with many questions,
  As we live and strive each day,
Trials, burdens, tribulations,
  Never seem to go away.
But we have this kind assurance,
  When we're founded on His love,
Faith shall never, never fail us
  For our Source is from above.

MEMORIES

Here I am well over sixty,
    Just an old man if you please,
With a lot of miles behind me
    And a world of memories.
Ev'rything has not been rosy
    Yet, I really can't complain,
What with life and all its problems
    I've been happy just the same.

I remember when Christ found me—
    It was quite a day for me.
I was bound by sin and shackled
    When, by Grace, He set me free.
I have never lost the feelin'
    When His Spirit touched my soul
In a moment—there He saved me.
    I was cleansed and then made whole.

Memories—I'll not forget them.
    I shall cherish them each day.
For the gift of my salvation
    I shall never cease to pray.
All the friends and all the loved ones
    That have been so kind to me,
And the reason all this happened
    Was because of Calvary.

How can I forget my Saviour
    Or the song "Amazing Grace"
Or the joy of sins forgiven
    When my past He did erase?
Lots of other things have happened
    But as long as time shall be,
For the day when I met Jesus
    That's—my Greatest Memory!

LAMPS IN THE NIGHT

I knew a pilgrim years ago
    Whose lamp was shinin' bright;
He was on fire for his Lord
    And walkin' in the Light.
He wore a smile of happiness,
    Contentment filled his soul;
And when he testified for God
    The Glory bells would toll.

It seemed that Heaven was so close
    When by his side you stood,
He was so friendly and so kind,
    So patient and so good.
He loved the Saviour and His Word,
    The tears would fill his eyes
When some poor sinner, lost, undone,
    From sin and shame would rise.

And then somehow a change took place,
    His smile had lost it's glow;
His love for Jesus disappeared,
    His lamp was burnin' low.
The cares of life they soon crept in,
    With storms and winds of doubt;
And in the darkness now he walks,
    No faith—his lamp is out.

I wish I knew the reason why
    This pilgrim lost his way,
And why his lamp of faith went out,
    And why he went astray.
I pray that God will keep my lamp
    All trimmed, and may it shine
To light the path that leads to home
    For this dear friend of mine.

THE ARKANSAS PREACHER

There's a preacher down in Akron,
In the State of Ohio,
Who is altogether diff'rent
From some others that I know.
Though he preaches in the City,
Let me tell you something' Pa,
He was born out in the country,
In the hills of Arkansas.

Now his preachin' isn't fancy
In the words of college men,
He just tells you plain and simple
That you must be born again,
And he doesn't try by wisdom
To convince you of your loss,
All he does is preach salvation
Through the Blood of Calv'ry's Cross.

You can tell that he's been sifted
By the Spirit as he talks,
And that he is dedicated
Even by the way he walks,
And when he gets into preachin'
And he shifts from low to high,
You just get so full of Glory
That you feel you're gonna fly.

Oh! I'll tell you when you're saggin'
And your Spirit's feelin' low,
Just to hear him preach salvation
Raises up your get and go.
This is what makes him so diff'rent,
Like his Momma and his Pa,
Who were called to preach the Gospel
From the hills of Arkansas.

BELIEVING GOD

After I had been converted
And from sin had turned away,
I was free and felt so happy
Ev'rytime I knelt to pray!
I just revelled in the Bible,
As I read it line for line—
Just to think, that ev'ry promise
I could claim by faith Divine!

Ev'rything I read was simple,
And as plain as plain could be;
It was just like God was speaking
By His word right straight to me.
Keep in mind, I had no learning,
Yet, somehow, God gave me light
To the Truth and Revelation—
What was wrong and what was right.

This, I think, has made the diff'rence
On this journey that's been long,
Trusting Him to lead and guide me
Even when there was no song.
I have scaled some little mountains,
Walked the valleys of despair,
Knowing God would never fail me
Or defeated—leave me there.

I've not needed men's persuasion
To believe what God has said,
Nor to fully trust my Saviour
For whatever lies ahead;
I'm determined more than ever,
Till I view that shining shore
Just to keep on God believing,
And to trust Him more and more.

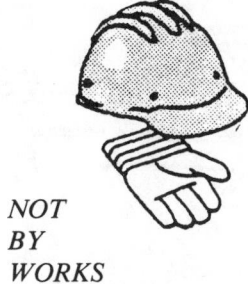

NOT
BY
WORKS

You can go to church each Sunday
  And at least twice through the week,
You can be a full time worker
  Or a deacon who can deke.
You may work just like a trojan
  And support most of the cost,
Yet, for all this going for you,
  You, my friend, could still be lost.

You don't work your way to Heaven
  Singing "Lover of my soul,"
Or because you lead the choir
  Or can make the organ roll.
These are far from God's credentials
  Like the clothes are to a man,
Not by works or by your merit
  Can you gain salvation's plan.

No, it isn't what you're doing
  Or how much you tithe or give,
No one ever bought salvation,
  It's a gift to all who live.
There is just one stipulation
  That applies to one and all,
We must have our sins forgiven
  And God's mercy on us fall.

Have you ever been to Calv'ry?
  This is where it must begin;
Taking Jesus as your Saviour
  And confessing all your sin.
And to rise a new born creature
  With salvation in your soul;
If you've never done this, neighbour,
  Then you've never been made whole.

WHY
ARGUE?

There was a time, I must admit,
  When I first saw the light,
I used to argue with those folks
  Who said I wasn't right.
I hope I didn't fail the Lord
  The way that I behaved,
But I just couldn't stand their talk,
  Who said I wasn't saved.

I'd travelled in the paths of sin
  And played the fool each day,
And for the pleasures of this world
  I dearly had to pay.
To satisfy my poor lost soul
  My life I'd freely stake,
Not knowing that I couldn't win;
  The odds were far too great.

It wasn't that I sought for fame
  Or wealth beyond my reach,
I only wanted to survive,
  Like clams upon the beach.
And yet, somehow I got caught up
  With things I thought were nice,
Until the day I met the Lord
  And claimed His sacrifice.

I've learned a few things through the years
  Since first I saw the light,
That arguing can never prove
  The things you know are right.
So now when someone doubts the Word
  Or tries to put me on,
Just short and sweet I take my stand
  And then I say "So Long."

MY TASK

The task the Lord has called me to
  May not appear to be
As big as some that others have,
  Or lesser by degree;
For if it is the Lord I serve,
  Then size does not reveal
That I am less important than
  The saint they call a wheel.

There's some whose task is mighty big,
  And some whose task is small,
For in the service of the Lord
  There's plenty room for all.
He knows just where we all fit in,
  And those who would be true
Rejoice in having just a share
  In things He'd have them do.

The wealthy saint don't have an edge,
  Nor those with pretty face,
For in His sight the thing that counts
  Is being in your place,
And with the talents that He gives,
  If five or two or one,
We all are judged within our class
  And by the job we've done.

So if my task appears quite small,
  And others big and great,
I'll have rewards like all the rest
  If I just pull my weight.
The most important thing to me
  Is not what others do,
It's being faithful with my task
  Until the journey's through.

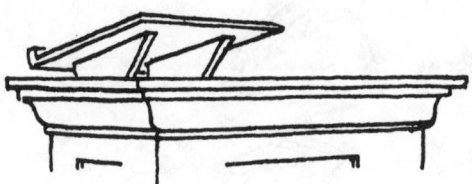

GOSPEL PREACHIN'

Once I thought to be a preacher
  All you needed was God's call,
And the Holy Spirit teach you
  Then His power on you fall.
But it seems that's too old fashioned
  For this changing world today,
Now to be a Gospel preacher
  You must have much more, they say.

Sinners now are much more wiser
  And much smarter in this day,
And that simple Bible preachin'
  Is too square for them, they say.
So if you would be a preacher,
  Of the Cross of Calvary,
You must learn to preach salvation
  With much more proficiency.

Well, I must admit it helps you
  When some church sends out a call,
And they see your robes of wisdom
  And diplomas on the wall,
But if you need all this learnin'
  Which today is quite a fad,
How did ever John or Peter
  Get along with what they had?

I don't want to hurt the feelin's
  Of those preachers of today,
Who have got so educated
  That you don't know what they say.
All I want is to remind them
  If they'll look around and see,
We need simple Gospel preachin'
  For the common folks, like me.

THE
LADDER
OF SUCCESS

To climb the ladder of success
    You've often heard them say,
It takes the best, and all you've got,
    There is no easy way.
The first few rungs are just a breeze
    But as you near the top,
That's when the goin' gets real tough,
    To win, you mustn't stop.

As you go up just keep in mind
    That someone must come down,
For at the top there's only room
    For one to wear the crown.
Someone must win, someone must lose
    In life's mad game we play,
Success is getting what you want
    At just what price you'll pay.

Some pay the price of all they have
    While striving for their goal,
And some I guess to gain success
    Have bargained with their soul.
To be successful may be great,
    Yet always keep in mind,
That happiness is more than all
    Success you'll ever find.

The ladder that is best to climb
    Is serving God each day,
And striving just to do His will
    Each step along the way.
And by His grace to reach for heights
    Of love and Holiness,
And all whoever reach these goals
    Find perfect happiness.

LIFE'S
AMBITION

All I've ever seemed to live for
    Since I've known redeeming love,
Is to witness for my Saviour
    And of Heaven up above,
Telling others of His goodness
    And the Cross of Calvary,
This has been my life's ambition:
    Serving Him who died for me.

Nothing else has really mattered
    As I've gone to work each day,
Other than to help some sinner
    Who like me had gone astray.
Singing of His love and mercy,
    Testifying of His grace,
Satisfied to be His servant
    With a smile upon my face.

Why should I want more than Jesus
    With His arms to hold me fast,
Or His promise to protect me
    Till the journey here is past?
Worldly pleasure, though alluring,
    With the treasures that they bring,
Lost their charm and their attraction
    When my soul began to sing.

Just to know Him and to love Him
    Has meant more than I can say,
Having Him to walk beside me
    Has brought peace and joy each day.
This has been my life's ambition
    Just to trust Him and to live
All my days to bring Him glory
    And all honour to Him give.

HIGHER
THAN
THE MOON

In this day of travel,
   Jumbo jets on high,
Astronauts and rockets
   To the moon can fly.
Though it's so exciting
   As they go their way,
I'm going higher
   Than the moon someday!

Soon I'll leave this planet
   For that Golden Shore,
Where there waits a mansion
   And a whole lot more.
Ev'rything is ready
   And I'm "A—O.K."
I'm going higher
   Than the moon someday!

I'll not need a space suit
   Or a rocket pad.
I'll not need a capsule
   Or be special clad.
All I'll need is Jesus
   When I go my way.
I'm going higher
   Than the moon someday!

Higher than the moon,
   Yes, higher someday,
Higher than the stars
   On the milky way,
To a place called Heaven
   Far beyond the sky,
Where I'll live forever
   In the bye and bye.

Oh, what a journey
   When I take my flight,
Walk the streets of Glory
   Dressed in robes of white.
I feel so happy
   Ev'rything's alright—Say!
I'm going higher
   Than the moon someday!

THE
BUS
BOYS

How about those gospel singers
   Trav'lling all across the land—
Wow! They really sock it to you
   With the fees that they demand!
All in air-conditioned buses
   And their wardrobes—what a sight
You can hardly tell the diff'rence
   From the night clubs—am I right?

These are pros at entertainment,
   All religious, that's for sure,
And to stop the poor free-loader
   They have ushers at the door.
It is really quite a business,
   Far beyond us little fry,
But you've got to give them credit;
   They're the best, you can't deny.

They've got agents and promoters,
   And each year they take a vote—
Who's the best and who's the greatest,
   Who can reach the lowest note.
And they even get so jealous
   Of each other and their acts—
That they'll try to rig the ballots
   If I understand the facts.

Now—If these are Christian singers,
   If they are—we've gone down-hill,
But I guess the world is changing
   Like the women and the pill.
So if you want entertainment
   By the greats and world renown,
Get your ticket at the wicket
   When the bus boys come to town.

THE UNSEEN PILOT

There seems to be a lot of folk
  Who say they would believe,
If God would only show Himself
  Or just a word receive.
They want some proof, a sign they say,
  Or maybe hold His hand,
They must be sure without a doubt
  Before they take their stand.

They have a right to live their lives
  The way that they believe,
For that's the way we all were born
  Since Adam was deceived.
We are the agents of our will
  Like ships out on the sea,
We chart our course. In other words,
  We choose our destiny.

Some choose to run their little ship
  As pilot, mate, and crew,
And where their journey's gonna end
  They haven't got a clue.
While others make the Lord their choice
  To chart and fix their goal,
And what a diff'rence in the trip
  When He is in control.

The storms of life are far too strong
  To battle ev'ry day,
Without this Pilot, though unseen,
  To safely guide the way.
And those who put their faith in Him
  And on His Word rely,
Shall anchor in the Port of God
  Forever, by and by.

WHO AM I?

Who am I to doubt the Bible
  And to say I don't believe
All the truth that God has written
  And His plan for man receive?
I'm a sinner just by nature
  And by all the things I've done,
This alone proves me unworthy
  Of His Grace and His dear Son.

I've no right to my opinions
  In the sight of God above.
Deep within I know my failures
  And how much myself I love.
Just because there are some statements
  That my mind can't figure out,
This gives me no right or reason
  God's integrity to doubt.

I'll be judged by Him—not people
  When I stand before His throne.
And my case, without a lawyer,
  I shall plead it there alone.
Not by works I've done or wisdom
  Shall I step down justified.
What I've done, by what is written
  This is how I shall be tried.

Who am I—I'm really nothing
  And by Grace I'll stand or fall,
I have taken Christ as Saviour
  And God's Word as all in all.
I believe it and receive it
  Ev'ry word and ev'ry line,
Who am I?—I'm just a sinner,
  Saved through faith by Love Divine.

FAILING FRIENDS

You're gonna lose a lot of faith
  In friendships here below,
When you find out how many fail
  Of all the friends you know.
Not ev'ryone who shakes your hand
  Will mean all that they say,
You'll find there's really very few
  Who by your side will stay.

The test will come when you're in need
  Of help along the road,
Of someone who will care enough
  To lift the heavy load
Of grief, and sorrow and despair,
  That never seems to end;
That's when you'll prove the ones you know
  Who said they were your friend.

You'll prove them all who really love
  You just for what you are,
Not what you were, or what you had
  When all your needs were par.
But when your world just falls apart
  And desp'rate is your need,
That's when you'll count them one by one,
  And few you'll find indeed.

But if your friends be few or more,
  There's one friend you should know,
The dearest and the truest friend
  You'll find on earth below.
The friend of friends, the Saviour dear,
  With grace and love Divine,
The only friend who never fails
  And He's a friend of mine.

WASTED TIME

When you think of all the effort
  That is wasted ev'ry day,
And the time we spend on pleasure
  On the games we like to play.
Nothing wrong in being happy
  Or enjoying what we do,
Yet, it won't have too much value
  When this mortal life is through.

All the trophies and the prizes
  And the medals that we've won,
All they'll be is dust collectors
  When our life down here is done.
All the time we've spent on pleasure
  And just building up our name,
Won't be worth a worn-out penny
  When we're no more in this game.

Life! Now there's a game worth trying;
  It's the greatest game on earth,
If you really think you've got it
  Here's the place to prove your worth.
Serving God and living daily
  With your eyes on Heaven's shore,
Storing up your future treasures
  Where there's pleasure evermore.

You will not become as famous
  When you live your life this way,
And you may not be invited
  To the functions of the day.
Yet, your time will not be wasted
  Or your effort been in vain,
When you spend them for the Master
  And not just on selfish gain.

TOO BUSY

We sing, "Take time to be Holy
   And speak oft with thy Lord"
When really what we ought to sing
   Is time we can't afford.
We're all so busy doing things
   And going here and there,
That if we really told the truth
   We've hardly time for prayer.

We're booked up solid ev'ry night
   And all day Sunday too,
We claim our time is on the line,
   To God we must be true.
And just to prove we want to serve
   Him well and do His will,
We run around, yet never learn
   To rest, or just be "still."

There was a day we spent more time
   To meditate and pray,
And how we'd wait upon the Lord
   Sometimes 'til break of day.
But somehow that has all been changed,
   Like cars that once had cranks,
For now we live as if we all
   Had tigers in our tanks.

We're livin' in a world gone mad,
   Where time has lost it's place,
And speed is making busy wrecks
   Out of the human race.
Yet, those who want to serve their God
   And all His will obey,
Don't let "too busy" get between
   The Lord and them each day.

THE OFFERING PLATE

In nearly ev'ry church you'll find
   Where people congregate,
The time will come and that's for sure
   To pass the off'ring plate.
And as it goes from row to row
   To do it's little chore,
It must feel awful sad at times
   When it returns I'm sure.

Imagine going row by row
   And empty you returned,
Not that you hadn't done your best
   But that your best was spurned,
I'll tell you if these plates could talk
   They'd have a lot to tell,
And if it ever went in print
   My, how those books would sell.

There's Mrs., well you know her name
   And Mr. so-and-so,
They're just about the sweetest folks
   That anyone could know.
But somehow when it's time to give,
   And help to pay the bills,
They sit there with that look of pain
   Like those who've got the chills.

It isn't that these plates would tell
   Of how much folks should give,
Or how some people run their lives
   Or how some others live.
It's only that they want to serve
   Where church folk congregate,
And come back smilin' to the front
   A well-filled off'ring plate.

WHO
IS
TO BLAME?

Man now can do most anything
  If he makes up his mind,
Because he's smarter than the rest
  Of animals you'll find.
The only thing about him is,
  With all the brains he's got,
He doesn't know how far to go
  Or when it's time to stop.

God gave us ev'rything that's good,
  As pure as pure could be,
But man has nearly ruined it
  And that is plain to see.
It seems men's brains get in reverse
  For often when they're through
They've done a lot more harm than good,
  We must admit that's true.

You only have to look around
  This world and see the mess
That men of brains have brought to us,
  Though they will not confess.
It's all their fault and that's no joke,
  Just check your list and see
The beauty and the good things gone,
  That once there used to be.

Among the names of those above
  There's some you'll never find
Who've made their contribution to
  The world and all mankind.
But those who've played with God's good earth
  And His creation plan
Should feel ashamed for all they've done
  To nature and to man.

REALLY
LOST—
FOREVER?

How can you say all the sinners
  Who have never read the Word
Or have never seen a Bible
  Or of Jesus ever heard,
Are condemned to Hell forever
  Without any hope or plea,
There to live in pain and torment
  In a dark eternity?

Are you sure—what you are saying?
  Can you prove it to be true
Not by your interpretation
  All what God is gonna do?
How do you know all the answers
  When it's only by His Grace
You and I have heard the Gospel
  And in Heaven have a place?

I know Jesus died and suffered
  To redeem those who believe,
And without His death at Calv'ry
  We no pardon would receive.
But to those who've lived in darkness
  Without one faint ray of light,
Do you think God will forget them
  Or refuse them what is right?

I don't want to use excuses
  When the Bible makes it plain
That your name must be there written
  And you must be born again.
Yet the more I read the Scriptures
  And somehow it seems to me
God will do what's right and honest
  When He hears—each sinner's plea.

70

A
BETTER
WAY

There's a better way of livin'
 Than this world can offer you.
And a better way of knowing
 What is always right to do.
You don't need to be a drifter
 If you want life at it's best,
All you need is God's salvation
 That will stand to ev'ry test.

You can't purchase it with money,
 It is free for you to own,
And it's yours for just the askin'
 In a humble sinner's tone.
If you want a song worth singin'
 And a hope for ev'ry day,
If you're willing to accept it,
 You can live this better way.

Peace and joy and many blessin's
 Are a few that you can know,
When the Saviour walks beside you
 As through life down here you go.
All the money, fame and glory
 Of a million millionaires
Couldn't touch this way of livin'
 For there's none with it compares.

This is life in all it's fullness,
 If you want it at it's best,
And the next will be much better,
 Heaven's joys and all the rest;
Life eternal safe forever,
 Without sorrow, grief or care,
And this life is found in Jesus,
 On your knees in humble prayer.

AUTHOR
OF
SIN

Some people say I'm crazy
 When I mention Satan's name,
And I tell them he's the author
 Of all strife, and sin, and shame.
Well, as sure as stars in Heaven,
 You had better get to know,
He's the one who got us started
 In the garden long ago.

He can trick you into sinning,
 For he knows where you are weak,
And when he has got you shackled,
 He'll display you like a freak.
He will strip you till you're naked
 Laugh and mock you with delight,
Then he'll drag you through the gutter
 Till you're just a hopeless sight.

He is after all the sinners
 For he wants us all in hell,
And the grave and outer darkness
 Are the wages he pays well.
Broken homes, with shame and sorrow,
 Drunks and all who live in sin,
Are the trophies that he offers
 And the prizes you can win.

I'm not crazy, friend and neighbour,
 Once I lived and served him well,
And if Jesus hadn't saved me
 I'd be on my way to hell.
Now when Satan comes to tempt me
 As he does from day to day,
I'm so glad I've got a Saviour
 Who can send him on his way.

71

AVAILABLE AND READY

Do you wonder why the Saviour
 Uses others and not you
In the cause of His great Kingdom
 Where there's so much work to do?
Maybe it's because your talent
 Never sees the light of day
And you're satisfied just knowing
 That your sins are washed away.

God expects His saints to serve Him
 And to show they love and care
For His grace and tender mercy
 And the blessings that they share.
There's a job for ev'rybody
 Who for Him would take their stand,
From the least unto the greatest
 We should be at His command.

Don't just sit around complaining
 That you're nothing—and too small!
Be available, and ready,
 Waiting for the Master's call.
Seek the Lord for His direction,
 Be committed to the task,
Give your best, however humble,
 That is all He'll ever ask.

Serving Jesus is an honour,
 It's the least we all can do.
There's so much to be accomplished
 If to Him we would be true.
Let us start to use our talents
 Like a beacon, let them shine,
As we strive as faithful servants
 You in your way, I in mine.

NO HELL?

Some people say there is no Hell,
 No Judgment Day ahead.
"This life is all there is," they say,
 "And when you're dead, you're dead."
The ones you find who talk that way,
 Are talkin' through their hat;
Or else God's Word is full of lies,
 And only fools say that.

There has to be a Judgment Day,
 If you will think it through,
For those who murder, cheat and steal,
 We're all included too.
There's no one who has played it straight,
 We all have fallen short,
And in the files of God above
 We've got a bad report.

No Judgment Day, no Hell, they say?
 My friend, don't be misled.
As sure as there are stars above
 You'll find out when you're dead.
There is a Judge who knows our past,
 And when our case comes up,
No crooked lawyers, bribes or lies,
 His Holy courts corrupt.

We'll stand alone and face the truth,
 For all the deeds we've done,
Unless we're saved and find God's grace
 Through Jesus Christ, His Son,
Who hung upon a cross of shame,
 While Judgment on Him fell,
To pay the penalty of sin,
 And save us all from Hell.

TELL IT LIKE IT IS

You have heard this modern saying,
"Why not tell it like it is?"
All the real and all the phony,
Without any froth or fizz.
If you want that information
Then the only source I know
Is the Word of God that's written,
That's the place where you should go.

There you'll find the truth untainted
And your ears may start to burn
When your questions have been answered
And the facts of life you learn.
God has never pulled His punches,
On His word you can rely
He's the only one who's honest
So—why not give Him a try?

You'll find out if you will trust Him
He has all you're looking for.
There is nothing you are needing
That He can't supply—I'm sure.
Ev'rything is clear and simple
Just as plain as earth and sod,
Without any tricks or nonsense
From the True and Living God.

Do you really want to hear it,
Like it is, without a lie,
How to get the best of living
Now and even when you die?
Calv'ry's love and full salvation,
God—and being one of His.
If you want it all in detail
In the Bible—there it is.

TRY PRAYIN'

When you wake up ev'ry day,
Try prayin';
When the skies are dark and grey,
Try prayin';
Tho' you've had a restless night,
And you look an awful sight,
Don't go seeking for a fight,
Try prayin'.

If you've never prayed before,
Try prayin';
Tho' at first your knees get sore,
Try prayin';
It's old fashioned, so they say,
Yet you'll find the more you pray
You'll be up-to-date each day,
Try prayin'.

When you're walking down the street,
Try prayin';
And some unkind friend you meet,
Try prayin';
Though you'd like to blow your stack,
See him fall flat on his back,
Don't just up and jump the track,
Try prayin'.

When you're feeling sad and blue,
Try prayin';
God still loves and cares for you,
Try prayin';
When you've lost your dearest friend,
And they say the world will end,
Trust in God, on Him depend,
Try prayin'.

WALKING
DEAD
MEN

Ev'ry time you meet a sinner
  Without life in Christ to claim,
Who has never been forgiven
  Calling on the Saviour's name,
You are seeing death in action
  For unless they know the Lord
They're as dead as anybody
  On the slabs down at the morgue.

Sure—they're walking and they're talking
  And they're breathing strange to say,
But they're nothing more than robots
  Satan winds up ev'ry day.
You will find them with the worldly
  With no hope or peace within—
Derelicts without direction
  And just skeletons of sin.

Most are very lovely people
  Just like me and just like you,
Who before we knew the Saviour,
  We were walking corpses too.
And it wasn't until Jesus
  Heard our plea and by His might
Lifted us from chains of darkness
  Gave us life and newborn sight.

Walking dead men—yes and women,
  Stained by sin and selfish pride
Without robes of God's redemption
  And a rebel's heart inside.
These are people we meet daily,
  And if Christ they fail to see
They'll be buried in their grave clothes
  Lost—for all eternity.

THAT'S
MY
CHURCH

Give me a church
  Where the Bible's read,
Where my soul can feed
  On the Living Bread:
And where mercy flows
  From the Fountain Head—
That's my church.

Give me a church
  Where they preach the word
Of the grace of God,
  And your soul gets stirred,
Where the Spirit works
  And His voice is heard—
That's my church.

Give me a church
  Where the saints can meet,
And where wealth and fame
  Cannot buy a seat;
And where no one's judged
  By the house and street—
That's my church.

Give me a church
  Where God's dearest Son,
Jesus Christ is Lord,
  And the risen one;
And where Heav'n is home
  When the day is done—
That's my church.

GOD
IS
DEAD!

There's been a lot of blasphemy,
  And many reasons why
The world is in such awful mess,
  And starving millions cry.
The latest really is the end
  Of all that has been said,
For now the Christ-rejecting crowd
  Say God in Heav'n is dead.

If God were living now, they say,
  These things could not exist,
Like want, and fear, and war, and hate.
  They do quote quite a list!
I listen and I think how sad
  To have a light so dim,
For placing all the guilt of man
  On God, and blaming Him.

God doesn't run this world my friend,
  For Satan's in command.
And that's the reason for the grief
  And trouble in the land.
The hordes of hell are now turned loose,
  Deceiving sinful men,
And things will go from bad to worse
  Till Jesus comes again.

You say God's dead? That's news to me,
  And just a lie I'd say,
For He was very much alive
  When I met Him today.
The facts are, if you want the truth,
  Is not that God is dead,
It's you who's dead and lost in sin
  And that's what God has said.

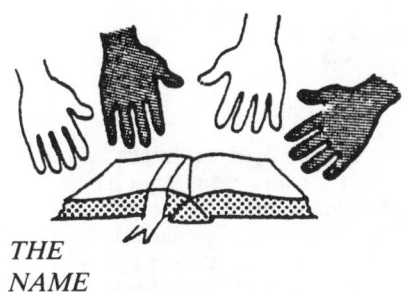

THE
NAME
OF THE GAME

Reaching out to those in trouble
  And to all who've gone astray,
Telling sinners of a Heaven
  And just how to find the way,
Sounding forth the precious message
  Without thought of any fame,
Livin' ev'ry day for Jesus—
  That's the name of this here game.

It's a game that's filled with kindness,
  Love, and help for all in need,
Giving hope to all the weary
  And a world that's hungry, feed.
Sacrificing time and money
  And the extra mile, go,
Proving that we care for others
  By the acts of good we show.

Not that works will ever save us,
  But I think it fair to say,
When you've met the Lord of Glory
  He expects you live this way.
Life takes on a brand new meaning
  In a world with so much need,
Faith and works, they go together
  And in Christ we shall succeed.

How we play this game of livin'
  Is a challenge to us all.
Are we ready "yes" to answer
  To the Saviour and His call?
Vessels, totally committed,
  Dedicated and aflame,
When you put it all together,
  That's the name of this here game.

GOD'S WHO'S WHO

There's a book on earth they tell me
    That contains the greatest names
Of the most important people
    Who have extra special claims.
Well—for sure my name's not in it,
    And I doubt the rest of you,
But it really must be something
    When you're one of those Who's Who.

Just to know that you are listed
    Here on earth with V.I.P.'s,
This must give you that strange feelin'
    That you get before you sneeze.
Without question there's exceptions
    Who deserve this high esteem
But some names I've heard them mention,
    Surely this must be a dream.

When the books above are opened,
    Filled with names of God's Who's Who,
Holy servants, men and women,
    Faithful martyrs, all the true:
Moses, David and the Prophets
    Joseph, Abraham and Paul,
Mary, Martha, John and Peter—
    God selected, one and all.

As for me I'll be so happy
    Just to make it through the gates
For I know I'm really nothing
    And deserve no special rates.
But I'll tell you one thing certain,
    When my work down here is through,
What a time I'll have up yonder
    When I meet all God's—Who's Who.

IF I BE LIFTED UP

If you want to be successful
    And to fill the church, they say,
Then you'll have to change the methods
    From the ways of yesterday.
Get yourself a real bright preacher
    With at least a few degrees,
And a board of good sharp deacons,
    Then the rest is just a breeze.

Have the choir sing a-go-go
    With that big way-out-there sound
And a musical director
    Who can really jump around.
Advertise in all the papers
    Hit T.V. and radio,
And a little touch of humour
    Always helps to start the show.

"Oh! and don't forget the building,
    Have it air conditioned too,
With the spotlights all in colours
    And the P.A. blastin' through.
Keep the sermon short and witty,
    Use the headlines of the day,
And keep ev'rybody happy
    If you want the crowds to stay.

Then when ev'rything is over
    And the doors have all been locked,
When the off'ring has been counted
    And the saints have all been shocked.
Some may criticize your methods
    Yet, you ought to feel quite proud,
When you tell the Lord in Heaven
    What it takes to draw a crowd.

GIVE GOD THE BENEFIT

Here on earth, there's many people
　　Filled with bitterness and doubt,
For like ev'ry unbeliever,
　　God—they still can't figure out.
So they fly right off the handle,
　　Baring all that's in their heart,
And they say a lot of mean things
　　As they tear our God apart.

They can't understand His wisdom
　　And they criticize His plan
From creation through the ages,
　　How He's dealt with sinful man.
And the thing that really sticks them
　　Like a car eight feet in mud,
Are His methods and His judgments,
　　Like ole Noah and the Flood.

He's a bully with no mercy,
　　And a lot more things they say.
As they keep on getting older
　　They get meaner every day,
And I guess the thing that burns them,
　　These accusers of His might,
Is the thought that, when they meet Him,
　　They'll find out that God was right!

There's a lot of links that's missing
　　In this mortal mind of mine,
And, to understand God fully,
　　I (like Him)—must be Divine.
So, when I can't comprehend Him,
　　Or His wisdom figure out,
I accept His word as final.
　　This, I find, removes all doubt.

NO REGRETS

Before I came unto the Lord
　　I say with much regret,
I did some crazy, foolish things
　　That I'd like to forget.
And yet as true as that may be,
　　One thing I must proclaim,
I've never had not one regret
　　That to the Lord I came.

The worldly crowd they soon were gone
　　With some dear friends I had,
While others in the fam'ly scoffed
　　And said that I'd gone mad.
It wasn't easy I'll admit,
　　To witness and be true,
For one just saved and born again,
　　With life in Christ so new.

Some told me that the Bible lied
　　And Christ was just a man,
While others claimed they had the truth
　　Of God's salvation plan.
To tell you that I got mixed up
　　Is just to put it mild,
And yet I stood upon the Word
　　And how those folks got riled.

I've no regrets He called me out
　　To walk the narrow way,
Or for the trials of the road
　　That I have had to pay.
The only one regret I have
　　That makes my eyes grow dim,
Is for the failure I have been
　　At times, in serving Him.

THE ETERNAL CITY

Have you heard about the city
  Without equal anywhere,
That will someday come descending
  Out of Heaven thru' the air?
It is larger than the cities
  Of this whole world all combined,
And has beauty, grace and glory
  No where else you'll ever find.

How I wish I could describe it
  With its palace and its throne,
Overshadowed by a rainbow
  Built of ev'ry precious stone;
Twelve foundations, walls of jasper,
  Onyx, chrysolite and beryl,
Ruby, topaz, agate, em'ralds,
  Gold and sapphire, gates of pearl.

Fifteen hundred miles and upwards,
  Fifteen hundred miles all square,
Built by God the great Creator
  For His saints with Him to share.
What a city! Oh, what splendour!
  Streets all paved with solid gold;
Words cannot express its beauty
  Or its majesty unfold.

I could tell you of the river,
  Tree of life, and so much more,
But I think I'd better tell you
  How to reach this golden shore;
Have your name inscribed up yonder
  In the book of life today,
Then you'll live with God forever
  In this city far away.

MY KINDA PEOPLE

Since I came to know the Saviour
  I have made some Christian friends;
Not the kind who only want you
  'Til your fame and money ends.
They don't have too high a ratin'
  With the crowd who live in sin,
But they are my kinda people,
  Sanctified, and born again.

They just love to talk of Jesus
  And to praise and testify;
And they're not ashamed to witness
  Of their faith in God on High.
They believe the Holy Bible,
  Not the modernistic crowd,
For they're satisfied and happy,
  And their prayers are clear and loud.

You won't find my kinda people
  Where the church is bottle fed;
Or if someone hollered 'Amen'
  That the preacher might drop dead,
But where God has got a servant,
  Though his helpers may be few,
Ev'ryday, they're hopin', longin'
  That the Lord will break the Blue.

Yes, I love these kinda people
  Who have found redeemin' grace,
Who are citizens of Heaven,
  And, someday, who'll take their place
With the saved of all the ages
  In the courts of God above;
I am proud that all these people
  Are the people that I love.

THIS WORLD AND I

This world and I were once good friends,
    Our ways were both the same;
We loved the things each other did,
    For life seemed just a game.
I played with sin like all the rest,
    And what a time I had,
Because I said, "I'll do my thing,"
    And I was hooked real bad.

But somehow, by the Grace of God,
    Salvation came my way;
I lost all int'rest in this world,
    And games I used to play.
The things of sin that had me bound
    With shackles that were tight,
Were broken clean when Jesus came
    And saved my soul that night.

This world and I are friends no more,
    It's ways are not for me;
The only purpose I have now
    To serve my Lord, you see.
He is my peace, my joy, my life,
    And all in Him I find,
I never knew such love before,
    Or Anyone so kind.

I've only got one longing now
    Until my God I see,
To trust His Word—and do His will
    And serve Him faithfully.
This world and I are through for good
    For Heaven is my goal,
I crossed the line—of no return
    When Jesus saved my soul.

RAISING CHILDREN

If you want to raise your children
    So they'll hate you when you're through,
Give them ev'rything they ask for,
    Never question what they do:
Don't correct them when they're cheeky
    Or their temper they display,
This will only hurt their feelings
    And they might just run away.

Let them have the car for dating,
    With your credit card to use,
Don't be harsh if you should catch them
    Using pot or drinking booze.
Let them butt in while you're talkin',
    Act as if it made you glad,
Be polite and just remember
    Who you are. Let's face it Dad.

Just because you pay to feed them
    And put clothes upon their back,
Just because you're out there workin',
    While they're back home in the sack,
This may once have given reason
    To exert or to complain,
But today the experts tell us
    Times have changed and love must reign.

Times have changed and that's no foolin',
    Kids are now well out of hand,
And us parents need remindin'
    That it's time to take a stand,
For if we don't change our methods
    Back to what they used to be,
We'll have children in the future
    Worse than these: just wait and see.

DON'T GROW WEARY

Just because you're few in number
  And your offerings are small,
Just because you seem to battle
  With your back against the wall,
Don't grow weary in well doing,
  Sure and great is your reward,
For your task is never little
  When you're working for the Lord.

Crowds don't prove that you're selected,
  And that God is pleased with you
Anymore than you're neglected
  When your numbers are a few.
If we count success by people
  And our blessings by a crowd,
Then I doubt if God is in it,
  Though it makes us feel quite proud.

Just a handful followed Jesus,
  If you read His Word Divine,
And not many walked beside Him
  When the chips were on the line.
And somehow I've got a feelin'
  That is hasn't changed today
From the time when our dear Saviour
  Walked this lonely pilgrim way.

Don't grow weary brother Christian,
  Fight the fight of faith, be true;
There's a prize for being faithful
  And a crown of Life for you.
Take your eyes off crowds and people,
  Get them on the Lord above,
And you'll find more joy in service
  On the road that leads above.

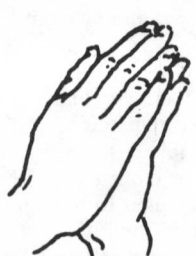

IT'S A SHAME

It's a shame how many people
  That I used to know and meet,
Who professed to love the Saviour
  And in Him appeared complete.
But today they walk the valleys
  Where there's death—and sinners moan
Strangers to the Grace of Heaven,
  And with hearts as hard as stone.

You can tell they're not too happy
  When you look into their face,
And you wonder what's the reason
  Why they turned on God's free Grace,
To go back to that far country,
  On the downward path be found,
Living on a sinner's diet
  Where the hogs and swill abound.

Could it be they couldn't take it,
  Living for the Lord each day,
With the Cross they had to carry
  And the price there is to pay?
Or did they become deluded
  With what others could afford,
And exchanged a hope eternal
  For the world and it's reward?

It's a bad—sad situation
  When you backslide and forget
All the pain that Jesus suffered,
  And you do not feel regret.
When you say you've changed your thinking
  And a Saviour's love disclaim,
Chances are you'll never make it
  And it really is—a shame.

GOD'S ELITE

You may never have great riches
  To afford the best that's made,
You may never once be cited
  As the tops in any trade.
Yet, if you are trusting Jesus
  And His death at Calvary,
You are classed with the Immortals
  In the Book of Life, you see.

You don't need to feel discouraged
  If the world gives you the air,
Or if you don't get invited
  Where the stars have got a chair.
They must have this praise and honour,
  With applause to make them smile,
Yet, the sadness of this glory
  Is, it's only for a while.

You and I who love the Saviour
  May have little rating here,
And the world may frown upon us
  Call us squares and think we're queer.
But regardless of our standing
  And the talent that we own,
You and I've got reservations
  To see Jesus on His throne.

That's the place to be invited,
  To the Palace of the King,
To enjoy His grace forever
  And where choirs of Angels sing.
Not because we were somebody
  Or in wealth we had a share,
But because we love the Saviour
  And He chose us to be there.

NEVER-ENDING FRIEND

Don't you trust a lot of people
  Just because they call you friend,
For you'll find a lot of people
  Who will fail you in the end.
Words are very eas'ly spoken
  When the sun is shinin' bright,
But they'll often change their meanin'
  When you're all alone some night.

In the darkness of your sorrow
  When you don't know where to start,
And when ev'rything collapses
  And your world has come apart,
Then you'll find how many people
  Will be there to hold your hand,
When you need a friend to help you
  Bear the load and understand.

Friends are just a dime a dozen
  When you're well and times are good,
And when ev'rybody's laughin'
  Like a crowd of good friends should.
But if fate should call your number
  Or when things go good to bad,
Then you'll find out those who love you
  And the friends you thought you had.

I have only met one stranger
  Whose been all a friend could be,
And He's never failed a moment
  Since He first befriended me.
Other friends are only human
  And sometimes their friendships end,
But all those who walk with Jesus
  Have a never-ending friend.

MY YESTERDAY

What has happened to the blessing
  That I once had in my soul
When I first received the Saviour
  And His blood had made me whole?
How I loved to read the Bible
  And to spend much time in prayer,
Jesus was my Lord and Master
  And His Presence I did share.

We would walk and talk together
  In such fellowship divine,
I was free, and Oh, so happy
  Just to know that He was mine.
What a friend, and what a Saviour!
  I was thrilled His love to know,
And to think for me a sinner,
  He to Calvary would go.

I don't now why things have altered
  And why I have lost my zeal.
Lord, I love Thee and adore Thee,
  And Thy Spirit is so real.
Yes, I know I'm getting older,
  And with problems that are mine,
Still, I need Thee to revive me
  By Thy grace and Love Divine.

Lord—I want that old time blessing
  That I once had in my soul,
And the joy of Thy salvation,
  Of my life take full control.
Nothing less is what I'm asking,
  As before Thee now I pray.
Where I've failed, dear Lord forgive me,
  Give me back my yesterday.

JESUS, WHAT A SAVIOUR

As I count my many blessings
  Like I do, from day to day,
I just marvel at the goodness
  Of my Lord along the way.
Peace and joy and full salvation,
  Life eternal—all are mine.
That's the reason I'm rejoicing
  In His grace, pure and Divine.

Not because that I'm so special,
  But because of His great love
And to know—I'm His forever,
  And my home is Heav'n above.
Just a mediocre person
  With such little fame to share,
Yet He deigns to walk beside me
  Ev'ry day I'm in His care.

It's so sweet to feel His Presence,
  He is with me where I go,
Ev'ry moment, ev'ry hour.
  What a thrill His will to know.
Such a kind and tender Shepherd,
  As He leads me on my way
I could never live without Him
  He is all my hope and stay.

What a Saviour—How I love Him!
  Ev'ry need in Him I find,
He has filled my ev'ry longing,
  Calmed my fears and restless mind.
For His mercy and His favour
  And for all He's done for me
I shall never cease to praise Him
  Now—and for eternity.

THE FAITHFUL

When I read the testimonies
  Of the higher personnel,
How they found they needed Jesus
  After they had done so well;
This is always quite a story,
  And it thrills me through and through,
When I hear God saves the famous
  Just the same as me and you.

Just imagine being someone
  With the world there at your door,
And a yacht to ride the ocean,
  Aeroplanes upon the shore,
Then to bow and get so humble
  As to want salvation's plan,
Makes me feel just good all over
  When I read of such a man.

This must take a lot of courage,
  After you have had your way,
And you've got all that you wanted,
  Brushing God aside each day;
Then when you have reached the portals
  Of the famous and the few,
There to find the goal you strived for,
  Full of wasted years for you.

Little wonder we start kneeling,
  When we've nowhere else to go,
As our sins rise up before us
  And the guilt begins to show.
Though it may be quite a story,
  Yet the thing I like to do
Is to read about the faithful
  Serving God their whole life through.

JUDGING

Don't you be a judge of others,
  How they praise and worship God;
If they clap their hands and holler,
  Though to you it may seem odd.
Or if they just sit and worship
  In a quiet sort of way;
You can't judge the faith of Christians
  By the actions they display.

Don't be hasty in your judgment
  Of the other fellow's way;
Just because you think you've made it
  And that he is still astray.
All have got the right to worship
  In the way that they believe,
In the way the Spirit leads them,
  As His leading they receive.

By your fruits shall all men know you,
  Are the words that Jesus said;
And He also said, Be careful
  Of the judgment path you tread,
Just because some worship quiet
  And the others shout and sing,
One cannot condemn the other
  For that doesn't prove a thing.

It is God who knows the intents
  Of the heart that loves His Son,
And the way we choose to worship
  Must be holy when it's done.
Our display in church may vary
  Like our days back to our youth,
But the way we all must worship
  Is in Spirit and in Truth.

CONVERSION DAY

There is one day I'll not forget
  As long as time shall be,
And that's the day when I was saved
  Through faith at Calvary.
I couldn't tell you what I prayed
  Or how salvation came,
I only know that since that hour
  I've never been the same.

It wasn't any fancy dream
  Or stupid man-made deal,
But God, by mercy and His grace,
  Made my salvation real.
And as I claimed the Precious Blood
  My Saviour shed one day,
The old life, with it's sin and shame,
  Was freely washed away.

The peace and joy and love that came
  Into this heart of mine,
Would take an Angel to explain
  With words of grace Divine.
It's lasted down through all these years
  With value more than gold,
It shall continue till one day
  The pearly gates unfold.

It was the day of days for me,
  And how I praise His name,
For saving my unworthy soul
  From all it's sin and shame.
Without a doubt, of all the days
  That ever came my way,
The greatest and the best I've known
  Was my conversion day.

WITHOUT EXCUSE

When you think of all the people
  That we have upon this earth,
Who have never heard the Gospel
  Of the Saviour or His birth,
Kinda makes you stop and wonder
  How a thing like this could be,
When we've got so many Christians;
  Boy, it sure does puzzle me.

Well, we may have had excuses
  In the days of long ago,
When the people had no money
  And when travel was so slow.
But today with jets to take us
  And when money is so free,
Seems we've either lost the vision
  Or it's just complacency.

Take the time and all the money
  That is spent to preach the word
To the same old crowd of sinners
  Who a thousand times have heard,
While the lost in heathen darkness
  Who can't buy a pair of pants,
Still have never heard the Gospel
  And to idols, prays and chants.

We may do a lot of talkin'
  How we love and serve the Lord,
And how much we love the sinner
  Who has never heard the Word.
Now we may have good intentions
  Yet the truth we can't deny,
While we live in need of nothing,
  Those without the Lord still die.

THE
CLEANSING
BLOOD

There's a lot of brand new products
  On the market now, I'm told,
That can make you look much younger
  Even when you're really old.
Yet with all their dyes and rinses,
  Creams and clays and beauty mud,
Nothing changes sin's complexion—
  Only Calv'ry's cleansing Blood.

Men can make you look so pretty
  With a dab of this and that,
Lift your face and hide your wrinkles,
  Keep you slim or make you fat.
There's no doubt you look much better
  When your frame they re-arrange,
But somehow that same old nature—
  This they never seem to change.

We all like to look exciting
  To our friends and all we see,
Yet to God looks don't impress Him,
  Nor our personality.
He can see beyond the make-up,
  Clothes and all the things we wear,
All the bought and artificial,
  Just as if they weren't there.

What He sees I guess is something
  That is better not to say
When we're down to bare essentials
  And to Him we're on display.
Beauty products may attract us,
  Like a cow that chews the cud,
But to God we look far better
  When we're washed in Jesus' Blood.

NOW
IS
THE TIME

It's about high time you listened
  To the news of saving grace,
And to stop and do some thinking
  When eternity you face.
Don't you think because you're busy
  With the other things you do,
That your plans will work out later
  When it's time for pleasing you.

You may think that when you're ready
  All you have to do is pray,
And the Lord will come arunnin'
  To your side without delay.
He's a million times too busy
  With the things He has to do,
To be treated like a puppet
  By the likes of me or you.

We've had far too many chances
  For a good excuse to find,
He has made salvation easy
  For the most of all mankind.
If we lived in heathen darkness
  Or our minds were void of use,
Then the story would be diff'rent
  And we'd have a good excuse.

Mark you well and underline it,
  Don't you play with saving grace,
For the time is coming, sinner,
  When the judgment you must face.
Then 'twill be too late for thinking,
  And too late for praying too,
If you don't take now the offer
  That the Lord is giving you.

GOD
FIRST

I've heard it said, if you will put
   God first in all you do,
That He will send both wealth and fame,
   And all these things to you.
I doubt that statement very much,
   And yet I could be wrong,
But I believe you'll find these things
   Held by the worldly throng.

God never pays in dollar bills
   For anything we do:
He does reward one here and there,
   But they are very few.
I know it says, "I will repay
   A thousand fold or more",
But those I know who put Him first
   Are far from rich. They're poor.

Let's face the facts and then we'll see
   The ones who put Him first,
If it be those with wealth and fame,
   And yet for more still thirst;
Or those who heard the Master's call,
   And went at His command
To do His will what'er the cost,
   Out in a foreign land.

No comforts there, no wealth and fame,
   No television shows;
No fancy cars, no luxuries,
   But burdens, trials and foes.
These are the ones who put Him first,
   I'm sure you will agree;
And tho' their treasure here is small,
   They'll reap eternally.

GOOD
OLD
TIME RELIGION

There's a lot of people sayin'
   That they're hopin' and
They're prayin'
   That for Heaven they are
Ready to depart:
   But they'll never make it neighbour,
If they haven't got the Saviour
   And that good old-time religion
   In their heart.

You don't need that hope-so preachin'
   Vain philosophy,
And teachin',
   God's redeeming grace and
These are miles apart.
   All you need to have salvation
Is a born-again sensation
   And that good old-time religion
   In your heart.

When you've got it, then you'll know it,
   And your life and face will show it,
All the gloomy past of sin
   Will then depart.
All your friends will hear you praisin',
   As your faith and joy keeps raisin'
With that good old-time religion
   In your heart.

That good old-time religion
   In your heart
That good old-time religion
   In your heart;
It will give you life anew,
   And a home beyond the blue,
That good old-time religion
   In your heart.

MY
REQUEST

When it comes for my departing
  From this world of sin and woe,
Please don't stand around me crying
  Or feel sad to see me go.
For you see—if I make Heaven,
  Like I'm hoping that I do,
I'll be really feeling sorry
  For the folks I've left (like you).

Just call up the undertaker,
  Ask him would he be so kind,
Come and pick up this ole body
  That I had to leave behind.
Don't go wasting any money
  Just to put me on display,
When the Spirit leaves this body
  What is left will just decay.

If some friends should come to see me
  Like a few I guess will do,
Why not treat them to some music
  And a Gospel message too?
This will give you much more pleasure,
  Play a record now and then,
Till it's time to close the casket
  And the Preacher says, "Amen!"

Really, I'll be glad to leave here,
  Though I surely can't complain,
But it seems I've been in trouble
  Ever since the day I came.
Don't feel sorry for me, neighbour,
  For with Jesus as my guide
I'll be safe with Him forever
  When I've reached the other side!

WHO
WAS
IT?

If it wasn't God, then tell me
  Who it was who made the earth,
And gives life to ev'ry creature
  That is born by ev'ry birth.
I'm just seekin' information
  To promote a worthy cause,
If it wasn't God of Heaven
  Then please tell me who it was.

See, I'm kinda plain and simple
  And I've got no axe to grind,
All I'm doing is just searchin'
  For the truth of this to find.
So if you have got the answer
  Then I'll listen, if it's true,
But you better not be guessin'
  Like a lot of people do.

Yes I've heard those many stories
  That the Bible isn't right
When it says that God created
  Ev'rything that comes in sight.
With the vast domain of Heaven,
  Far beyond what eyes can see,
So if God is not creator,
  Who would you say it would be?

Would you care to name the person
  Or the way it all began,
All the earth and all the planets,
  How they came along with man?
As for me I'll trust the Bible
  Though to some it may sound dim,
No one else but God could do it,
  Ev'rything was made by Him.

87

MAKE SURE

If your mind is set on Heaven,
  Let me give you my advice:
Don't take anything for granted,
  Though it may sound awful nice;
When you hear somebody preachin'
  On the way and how to go,
Better check it with the Bible
  And make sure that it is so.

There are many ways to Heaven—
  Well, at least that's what men say,
And this world is full of 'isms'
  That will lead you far astray;
Don't rely on man's opinion,
  Or the sermons that you've heard;
Only if you know for certain
  That it's written in God's Word.

Don't let anyone deceive you,
  For there's far too much at stake;
All eternity before you,
  After death when you awake;
So you see it's so important
  That you know without a doubt,
That your soul has got salvation,
  And your sins are blotted out.

Now I don't profess much wisdom,
  And my learnin' ain't been great,
But I'll tell you something, neighbour,
  I would never hesitate
To put all my faith and callin',
  And forever take my stand,
On the Word of God that's written,
  And not on the word of man.

UP-TO-DATE RELIGION

There's a brand of new religion
  That they're pushing hard today,
It's the lowest of the many
  That the pit has sent this way:
It denies the inspiration
  Of the Holy Written Word,
With the Virgin birth of Jesus
  Only fiction and absurd.

What gets me is how they know it—
  That the Bible is untrue,
Could it be that they're much wiser
  Than the likes of me and you?
Or are they just only talking
  With their big mouths open wide,
And are trying to impress us
  From the hate that burns inside?

If they had some news to tell us
  That we'd never heard before,
Or some proof to even show us
  Then we'd listen, that's for sure.
But it's only just another
  Form of Satan's bold attacks
By his cohorts to deceive us
  From the truth and Bible facts.

New religions come and vanish
  Like the men that bring them in,
But the truth that's in the Bible
  Still is truth, and sin is sin.
We don't need no new religions
  For there's nothing new to find,
All we need is more believing
  In the good old fashioned kind.

CRUTCH RELIGION

Ever hear those worldly sinners,
  Those who think they know so much,
Say religion is to lean on,
  Just the way you would a crutch?
That's alright if your religion
  Is too weak to make you stand,
But when you've got God's salvation
  All your strength is in His hand.

When your soul has been converted
  And you're saved and cleansed inside,
All the systems of religion
  That are sick are left outside.
You are now a new creation
  Full of faith and peace and love,
And in sickness, health and sorrow
  All your help is from above.

If you need a crutch to lean on,
  As these sinners often say,
Then I doubt if your redemption
  Was received the Calv'ry way.
All you need to have and hold you,
  If you love the Saviour dear,
Is a faith that will not waver
  And a trust that knows no fear.

When you talk about religion
  Being just a crutch to use,
Are you sure you're not in darkness
  And you need a stronger fuse?
Get a Holy Ghost salvation
  And a Saviour who is strong,
Then you'll need no crutch religion
  Once you've joined the ransomed throng.

THOSE ODD CHRISTIANS

Those Christian folk are not too bright,
  That's what the critics say;
We're just a crazy mixed up crowd
  Whose minds have gone astray.
Imagine singin' gospel songs
  And prayin' day and night;
I guess we do seem odd to those
  Who never saw the light.

And when you think of how we live
  By faith from day to day,
And always turn the other cheek
  And all our debtors pay,
To do the things we know are right,
  Be kind to all we know,
And when somebody fails our trust,
  The love of Jesus show.

And then forgive our enemies
  And go the extra mile,
Be ready with a helpin' hand
  And always wear a smile.
No wonder we appear quite odd
  To those who live in sin,
You just can't help but live this way
  When you've been born again.

We may seem odd and all mixed up,
  To some we may seem queer;
But little do they realize
  Our home is far from here.
We're pilgrims in a foreign land,
  And though we may seem odd,
It's no disgrace to do what's right
  And live to please our God.

GOSPEL IN MUSIC

Don't you think that Gospel singers
  And musicians of the Lord
Should be saved and dedicated
  Same as preachers of the Word?
I believe we need the Saviour
  If we're singing Gospel songs
Either that or else we're standing
  In a place a saint belongs.

You may fool the folks that listen
  For you'll find most of them there
Are just ordinary people
  And as critics—only fair,
But you've got yourself to live with
  And remember as you sing
That the Gospel—words and music
  Is no big top circus thing.

Jesus bled, and died, and suffered
  Pain—unheard of and unknown,
Without any help or comfort,
  And He did it all alone.
So be careful how you praise Him,
  Making sure your lips are clean
And your life in Him is hidden,
  And to Calvary you've been.

I'm not down on Gospel music
  For to me—next to the Word
It's the sweetest sound the ransomed
  Here on earth have ever heard.
All I say—we owe the Master,
  If of Him we sing and play,
Is to know Him and to serve Him
  With our sins all washed away.

GIVING YOUR BEST

Life seems to me just like a race,
  We all start out the same,
We're naked born, then get a tag,
  A number and a name.
They weigh us up and wash us down,
  In flush-a-bye's we rest
Until it comes to feeding time
  Then what a howling test.

We grow up and it's still the same,
  We struggle for the top,
And many times we blunder on
  And wind up just a flop.
But one thing we must all agree,
  We'll practice and rehearse,
Determined to put out our best
  For self, we must be first.

The story just keeps going on
  Until it's God we serve,
Instead of giving Him our best,
  That place we still reserve.
We often give Him just the crumbs
  Of time we have to spare
And wonder why our lives are flat
  Like tires without air.

This Christian race includes us all,
  The weak as well as strong.
No matter where in line we stand,
  Our best to God belongs.
It is no shame to not be great
  Like some I could suggest,
But if it's God you say you love
  Then He deserves your best.

THE
LIFE
THAT COUNTS

The life that counts the most for God
  Is easy to assess,
It is a life of perfect trust,
  A life of faithfulness;
All other things just fall in line
  Like night that follows day,
When we surrender all to Him,
  And all His will obey.

It's not an easy life, that's true,
  For sinners to resign
From all the pleasures of the world
  And walk by Faith Divine,
And yet it pays a thousand fold
  With peace and joy within
To know your life is pleasing God,
  And that you're free from sin.

This life in Christ is meant for all
  The Saints like me and you,
But only God knows those of us
  Whose life is always true.
Most of us have to hang our head
  When we are all alone,
And on our knees admit to God,
  Our hearts are hard as stone.

Oh, Lord, for life that has no shame,
  And love to fill my heart,
Give me this life my Saviour dear
  And all the world depart,
Until I live for pleasing Thee,
  A life of faith each day,
A life that counts the most for God
  In all I do and say.

HOW HARD
HAVE
YOU TRIED?

Friend, if you don't mind me asking
  There's one thing I'd like to know
Would you like to go to Heaven
  When you're finished here below?
If you would, you need the Saviour,
  With the Cleansing Crimson Tide,
Now if this is what you're seeking,
  Just how hard then have you tried?

Have you ever made an effort
  To believe, and faith to share,
Or to kneel down at an altar
  In humility and prayer?
Surely this is not much asking
  To be free and justified,
If you really want salvation,
  Just how hard then have you tried?

God don't want some great big favour,
  Or some mighty deeds from you;
You don't have to prove you're worthy
  Or you're fit to make it through.
Just a word in true repentance,
  And in Jesus to abide,
This is all, and if you want it,
  Just how hard then have you tried?

Tell me what will be your answer
  If you fail to reach that shore
When you knew you could have made it
  And had chances by the score:
One thing certain, you'll regret it
  Then, unless you now decide,
If you haven't got salvation,
  Just how hard then have you tried?

GOD'S AMBASSADORS

There isn't anyone, I guess,
  Who wouldn't like to be
The President of some great land
  Or noble Royalty.
And yet as fine as these jobs are
  And high as they may stand,
The highest calling is to serve
  Christ in a heathen land.

To leave your home and all that's dear
  And take the precious Word
Across the seas to foreign shores
  Where souls have never heard.
To tell them of a Saviour's love
  And battle Demon pow'r,
There is no work demands so much,
  Each day and ev'ry hour.

To walk through jungles all alone
  Where dangers always hide,
With only faith to see you through,
  An Angel as your guide.
And still press on to reach the lost,
  Though often filled with fear,
And in the stillness of the night
  With faith that God is near.

It takes the love and grace of God
  To fall upon a soul,
To have them choose the mission field
  And claim it as their goal.
There is no greater, higher job
  With rich eternal gains,
Than being God's Ambassador
  Where heathen darkness reigns.

TIME AND EFFORT

It takes time and it takes effort
  When you start to serve the Lord
In a life of dedication
  That must meet with His accord.
So be careful when you're praying
  That you mean the things you say
For you'll find if God should call you
  He'll expect your best each day.

Serving Him is not that easy
  You will find it's quite a task
And sometimes the job that's given
  Might seem more than you have asked.
Once your life has been committed
  You'll have nothing more to say
Than to ask God for direction
  For each step along the way.

He won't take no lame excuses
  If the job is poorly done,
He wants total preparation
  When we represent His Son.
Heaven's best He gave to save us
  And His Grace that we may learn
So you see—it's only fairness
  He "our all" wants in return.

Not that we can pay for Jesus
  Or the Debt of Calvary
Nor for life that is eternal
  That by Faith can set us free.
But as servants true and faithful,
  Once you say—"Dear Lord I'm Thine"
If you meant it—then you'll prove it
  By your effort and your time.

SOUL SEARCHING

Ev'ry now and then we Christians
  Who are saved and love the Lord
Should be taking inventory
  Of our stock within the Word.
If we don't—then we are liable
  To grow cold and lose the thrill
And the joy of God's salvation
  Purchased there on Calv'ry's Hill.

We need more than church attendance
  Or just sitting in a pew
To encounter all the trials
  That this world can put you through.
We need quiet times with Jesus
  Underneath His Holy Light,
Checking out our lives and motives—
  Are they pleasing in His sight?

Is our prayer life up to standard?
  Just how much the Word we read?
Do we have a clear-cut witness?
  Is there any hate or greed?
Is our talking pure and honest?
  Are we known by those we see
To be up-right Christ examples
  Striving more like Him to be?

You may think it's not important
  To be "still" and check your list,
But if you take all for granted
  You are bound God's best to miss.
You and I can't face the burdens
  And the toiling of the day
Unless we spend time with Jesus
  In an inventory way.

MARKS OF CHRISTIAN WRITING

If you want to be a writer
  Of a poem or a song,
Or if you would write a story
  Ten or twenty chapters long,
Now I hope you're not discouraged
  After hearing what I say,
For unless you're called to do it
  You'll just waste your time each day.

Gospel writing isn't easy,
  It takes effort, time and prayer,
And when once you've got the burden
  You will have no time to spare.
Other things that seemed important
  You will freely sacrifice,
For to be a Christian writer
  Hours of labour is the price.

Just remember words are precious
  And their value more than gold,
And the message of salvation
  Must be simple when it's told.
And when this thought grips your spirit
  And the whole world comes in view,
Then you'll understand why writing
  Must have all the best of you.

Prayer for guidance and for wisdom
  You must ask the Lord to give,
And each word to have His blessing
  And His truth to make them live.
Now if this is your desire
  And the call should come your way,
All your writings for the Saviour
  Will be blessed of God each day.

SOUND ADVICE

Write a poem, will you, poet;
　　Let me know what's in your heart.
Give me truth, and give me wisdom,
　　Set the good and bad apart.
Talk in language plain and simple
　　Let me know what road to take,
Give me warning of the pitfalls
　　And in life what is at stake.

Don't dream up some fancy thinking
　　That is soothing on the mind;
Let me have the facts of living,
　　What is real—no phony kind.
If there's anything worth knowing,
　　Please don't hesitate to tell.
Give it straight and don't be guessing,
　　Earth and Heaven—even Hell.

Well, you've asked for quite a portion,
　　So I'll do it as you said
Plain and simple as I know it
　　From the cradle 'til you're dead.
It's survival of the fittest,
　　Spirit, body, soul, and mind,
And there isn't one exception—
　　Happiness is hard to find.

You'll know loneliness and sorrow,
　　Deep frustration, grief and tears.
Life is not a lovely journey
　　If you're lost with guilt and fears;
But there is a diff'rent story
　　If the Bible you will read
There you'll find a loving Saviour
　　Who shall fill your ev'ry need.

THE NOW GENERATION

Youth today, in my opinion
　　Are about the same I'd say
As in other generations
　　And in ev'ry other way.
Only diff'rence are the parents
　　Who have failed to take command,
And have let the kids grow wild
　　Like a bull that's out of hand.

Now they want the facts and reasons
　　Nearly from the day they crawl,
And they blossom into season
　　When their brains are far too small.
We have let them be the bosses
　　And the truth is nothing less
Than a fouled up generation
　　That is really in a mess.

Rock and roll with sex and hippies,
　　Marijuana, L.S.D.,
Love-in, sleep-in, all together,
　　Doing what comes naturally.
God forbid that I should judge them,
　　But if we still compromise,
All these kids will soon despise us,
　　If us parents don't get wise.

What's the answer? Why that's simple,
　　If we want it honestly.
Train a child, says the Bible,
　　Up to what it ought to be:
Give them lots of love and kindness,
　　But if this should fail to stand,
Get the rod and beat their breeches
　　Till they know whose in command.

THE DAY
THE
WELL RAN DRY

O'er the years we've had our troubles,
   What with sorrow, pain and care,
And sometimes some friends have failed us,
   Made our grief so hard to bear.
But with all our disappointments
   That at times have made us cry,
It was worse, and more depressing
   On the day the well ran dry.

That old well had never failed us
   And its water was the best.
It was always so refreshing,
   Never knew an unfit test.
We forgot how much its value,
   As we taxed its good supply,
It was then we learned our lesson
   On the day the well ran dry.

We had gone about our business
   Without any thought each day
That the source of our existence
   Could be taken right away.
Yes, we did a lot of prayin'
   Told the Lord about our need.
It was good to know He heard us
   And to see Him intercede.

You and I have much in common,
   There are times we lose our way
As we take our God for granted
   And His love from day to day.
Though He knows our ev'ry weakness
   He is always standing by
With His well of grace and mercy—
   And it never shall run dry.

I AM
A
CHRISTIAN

I am a Christian . . .
   Redeemed from a fallen race
Of lost sinners,
   By faith in the death and
Resurrection of Jesus Christ
   At Calvary.
I pledge my Allegiance
   Shall ever be to my Saviour and God,
The God who created Heaven and earth,
   The faith of our forefathers
Shall I keep, and cherish,
   And uphold with steadfast loyalty.
The Holy Bible shall I treasure
   And all its truth defend and place
Above all my possessions, ambitions,
   Pride and moral integrity.
By the grace of God
   I shall accept sufferings, scorn,
Reproach, loneliness, and all
   Trials of this world as an
Obligation to the sacred trust
   That is mine.
I am a Christian . . .
   A joint heir with Jesus Christ:
Heaven is my eternal home.
   God helping me,
In humility and gratitude
   I shall fulfill, from this day,
With joy, my responsibility
   As long at I live.
I am a Christian.